Find your
queen!

Arem Estill
Taylor

WWII
THE NATIONAL
WWII MUSEUM

PHANTOM FATHER

A DAUGHTER'S QUEST FOR ELEGY

SECOND EDITION

SHARON ESTILL TAYLOR, PhD

Cover Art: Adam Surrey, www.facebook.com/ghostoftime
Author Photo: Sylvia Watson, Hardt Photography, www.sylviahardt.com

ISBN–13: 978-1-945431-21-0

Printed in the United States of America.

This publication is designed to provide entertainment value and is sold with the understanding that the publisher is not engaged in rendering legal, accounting, or other professional advice of any kind. If legal advice or other expert assistance is required, the services of a competent professional person should be sought.

—From a Declaration of Principles jointly adopted by
a Committee of the American Bar Association and a
Committee of Publishers and Associations

PRAISE FOR PHANTOM FATHER

"The true heroine of the saga, however, is Sharon Estill Taylor, who was all of three weeks old when her father was shot down during WWII. Sharon has spent a lifetime searching for her dad."

—October 9, 2006 news release
from the United States Department of Defense

"It's such a powerful story and reflects well your devotion and persistence in telling this story of your love for your father and of the continuing bond."

—**John Harvey**, editor of the *Journal of Loss and Trauma*
and professor of psychology, emeritus, University of Iowa

"Thank you for sending this beautiful story to me. Your writing is so lovely and lyrical—you are a wordsmith. This piece is breathtaking, heartbreaking, and heartwarming by turns. I was in awe—and then I was in tears."

—**Margaret Ann Comito**, MFA, memoirist

"The people you have met, the experiences you have had—you are so very capable of bringing it all together to tell your father's story. How very proud your dad will be someday to meet his precious daughter."

—**Marjie Collins**, wife of WWII P-38 fighter pilot
1st Lt. Don Collins

For my three parents, who are the constant stream running beneath my life

For Hans-Guenther Ploes, my partner in making the impossible possible
(Sie haben meine ewige Dankbarkeit, Dumbo)

For my Owen, who encouraged me to write this second edition, along with a second edition of us

Mine is not a story of grief but of yearning—
lifelong and incremental, deep and pervasive,
breath-catching and constant, just out of
touch, yet a lurking presence. It's having
a small, sad girl's hand in your own. She is
watchful as she keeps her vigil throughout
each day and night. She is the architect of the
path she walks to meet her phantom father.
Hers is a daughter's singular journey.

—Sharon Estill Taylor

«The elegy does the work of mourning. It allows us to experience mortality. It turns loss into remembrance and it delivers an inheritance. It opens a space for retrospection and drives wordless anguish, wordless torment toward the consolations of verbal articulation and verbal ceremony. Many of us carry the dead around with us. We shouldn't feel ashamed of that.»

—Poet Edward Hirsch, author of the book-length poem *Gabriel*

FOREWORD

In November 2008, I was invited to speak at the American War Orphans Network (AWON) Conference in Tucson, Arizona. It was a privilege to be invited to attend their bi-annual gathering and humbling to be in the presence of hundreds of men and women that had lost their fathers during World War II.

My purpose in attending the conference was to share the vision for The National WWII Museum in New Orleans, Louisiana. In 2008, we were in the early stages of a $400 million expansion that would create a museum dedicated to the American experience in World War II, telling one of the most important stories in human history through the lens of why the war was fought, how it was won, and its meaning decades after the fighting had ended.

My session was scheduled mid-morning, and it followed a moving presentation made by an AWON member who had recently found the site of her father's plane crash. That member was Dr. Sharon Taylor, and over the course of her presentation, she took us with her on a journey of love, tenacity, and perseverance that ultimately led to her finding and bringing her father, 1st Lt. Shannon Eugene Estill, home. There wasn't a dry eye in the room.

Since our meeting in 2008, Sharon has made tremendous strides in sharing the story of finding her father and has been a passionate advocate for the ongoing mission of the Defense

POW/MIA Accounting Agency, which is still actively working to "provide the fullest accounting for our missing personnel to their families and the nation." With more than 81,000 Americans still missing from World War II and later conflicts, there is still much work to be done.

At The National World War II Museum, we are proud to have been part of bringing Sharon's powerful story to a broader audience. In 2010, we premiered *A Love in the Time of War: The Last Flight of Lt. Estill*, the documentary chronicling Sharon's journey to find her father, and in 2016, Sharon presented at our International Conference on World War II. In 2018, Sharon's passion for our mission took on even greater meaning when she joined the Museum's board of trustees, helping ensure that we continue our journey to complete America's National World War II Museum and provide educational programs for current and future generations.

The story of Sharon and her father is remarkable and complex, and one you will get to know in detail in *Phantom Father: A Daughter's Quest for Elegy*. It was also the impetus for a great friendship, built on our mutual passion for honoring the men and women who fought for our freedom in World War II.

Thirteen years since our initial meeting in Tucson, *Phantom Father* is now in its second edition, and at The National World War II Museum, we are in the final stages of completing our campus. These accomplishments are a testament to the enduring lessons and legacies of World War II. I hope you will be inspired by what you read in the coming pages and come see us in New Orleans soon.

With gratitude,
Stephen Watson
President and CEO
The National World War II Museum
April 2021

SECOND EDITION
AS CODA

For more than a decade, I have been privileged to bear witness to the growth of the National WWII Museum along with the people and events it celebrates. I have been able to watch the past being faithfully recreated and work with others to ensure the museum's future. Publishing the first edition of this book in 2016 resulted in my parents' WWII letters coming to reside within the very heart of the museum.

Thus, this second edition is a coda. By definition, a coda is "a concluding part of a literary work, a summary at the end of further developments in the lives of the characters." When I finish a book, I savor the coda or miss its absence. It's a soft landing at the story's end that takes the reader into the future of "then what happened."

Since I see the intervening years since first publication as a continuum rather than a closure, I offer this coda as an updated and renovated version of the first book. Above all, 1st Lt. Shannon Estill has a place in history where his story is told and remembered. That was my intention all along.

Dr. Sharon Estill Taylor
May 2021

TABLE OF CONTENTS

A PRELUDE

As a child, the moments I felt closest to my father usually unfolded over a chocolate malt at Woolworth's lunch counter. My paternal grandmother and I would share a single towering milkshake—always poured from the silver container into a thick fountain glass topped with a generous twirl of whipped cream, three cherries, and two fat straws. I would ask my Nana Lettie to tell me about the father I never knew: her eldest son, 1st Lt. Shannon Eugene Estill. His fighter plane was shot down three weeks after I was born, just as WWII ended. Tears welled in her eyes as she told me about the dashing young fighter pilot who died for his country during one of the war's darkest hours.

I'm not sure why we reserved our heart-to-heart talks for Woolworth's lunch counter in downtown Enid, Oklahoma. Perhaps it was the one time we could talk, just the two of us, girl to girl, while my grandfather waited for us at home. Perhaps it was the mindless chatter and laughter of other patrons who served as a backdrop for our conversations.

In any case, Nana Lettie made it a point each time to balance her audible grief with one certainty: "You will always be your daddy's little girl," reminding me that her son left me for her to love. Nana promised that my father's benevolence surrounded me, just as he surrounded her. Whenever she found a good parking place in the town square, she attributed her good fortune to him.

These moments at Woolworth's with my Nana fascinated and terrified me in equal measure. While bearing witness as her invisible pain became tearfully visible, I could believe my father loved me as much as she said he did.

The more I heard my Nana Lettie tell me about the father I would never know, the more I wanted to change our fate and take away her sadness. With hopeful enthusiasm, I announced, "I will find him and bring him home!" I had no idea how a seven-year-old hoped to accomplish this task, but a promise was made. This is the story of how I kept it.

AN INTERRUPTED DAUGHTER WITH PRETEND FRIENDS

The first time I dared to express myself about my dead-in-the-war father was in Pillsbury School kindergarten in northeast Minneapolis. I drew my version of an A-bomb and proudly printed my name on the back of the paper. When we held up our drawings, I was the only one who claimed to have drawn the bomb that killed her daddy.

Prior to the A-bomb incident, I was considered, according to my kindergarten report card, a "vivacious, happy child, cooperative, alert, eager to please, very talkative, enjoys all phases of kindergarten, follows directions well, handwork excellent, and gifted with a sense of rhythm and song."

Despite these glowing classroom endorsements, my teacher recommended to my parents that I visit a child psychiatrist. I blamed the bomb drawing but knew that my growing relationship with a cadre of pretend friends and an acquired Boston/English accent were also on the table. Add that to nose bleeds and a fear of bats—which actually flew around the ceiling of my room in our first house, producing night terrors—to the list of my emerging psychosis. I was supposed to be all those words on my kindergarten report card, not sitting in a doctor's office for drawing a bomb. Everyone seemed more interested in hearing about my frequent (imagined?) visits from my father, Shannon Eugene, who appeared in uniform standing in my bedroom. The effort to suppress my grief and curiosity had begun.

What I wasn't saying was that when my new daddy came along, the recipe of my life changed, as great heavy globs of starch were added. The same Niagara Instant Laundry Starch in which my mother dipped my new father's dress shirts, before rolling and refrigerating them overnight. She would iron them throughout the next day and stand them up all over our narrow house. Drinking Coke from an icy, green bottle as she ironed was part of the routine. I was allowed a sip, but not a bottle of my own. I sat nearby with my books, telling her stories I'd memorized from the illustrations. She played her music on a record player, which meant she had to change or turn over the record every shirt or two. She said my new daddy didn't want to pay a laundry bill when she was so good at doing his shirts.

We moved from our first house across from the big Catholic church near my new daddy's store, into a duplex apartment, which was nearer the school where I would attend kindergarten. Parental logic borne of having one car and a mother who hesitated to ride in a car, much less drive one, relocated us. I was happy to escape the bats in my old attic bedroom. It was there that scarlet fever cracked open my young consciousness to the possibility of monsters. The bats didn't help, nor did the tension created by my mother in her dance with my new daddy, who liked to tell her to stop thinking about the past.

When we moved, I discovered a minor stable of pretend friends who lived with me behind the folding screen that served as my "bedroom." The screen partitioned off a corner of the dining room that shared the wall of my newly married parents' bedroom. I had pretend friends as tenants in every corner of my folding screen retreat. They sat on my bed, settled themselves around the screen hinges, hovered on the headboard, and snuggled among my books and toys. Eugene, my favorite, would simply lean against the wall, all crisp and clean in his khaki shirt tucked into his khaki pants, met in the middle by a khaki belt with a shiny brass buckle. His buttons matched his shirt exactly, and he was always smiling, arms crossed. I loved him for that. His was the attitude of the already-lost 1940s—a man home from war. When I told my mother I saw him and talked to him, she just said, "Yes, honey, isn't that nice?"

Each night, as we waited for my new daddy to come home from the Woolworths store where he was the manager, I asked my mother to set places at the dinner table for Eugene and two girls—Maydris (retrieved from a character called Maytah in my mother's radio serial, *The Guiding Light*) and a watery female persona with the unlikely name of Apricot. My mother humored me. My new daddy did not.

Mom convinced me that only one could join us at a time due to space restrictions at a four-place table and the fact that she only had three sterling silver engraved napkin rings. We bought them at Dayton's department store silver department in downtown Minneapolis. We took the streetcar to get there, and people complimented me on my pretty red hair all along the way. She wanted the napkin rings engraved, so it took two trips. My new daddy's napkin ring matched hers, oval with simple initials. Mine was a bunny and carved with my new initials. Out with my "E" last name initial, in with a bolder "R." As always with adoption, everything was erased and rewritten. When someone is adopted, the puzzle pieces are thrown down, and everyone walks away. The adopted one is left with the pieces to two different puzzles. That was me.

My pretend cohorts would take their turns at the table where their places were set. I shared my sterling silver napkin ring with the bunny on it with those selected. It was the least I could do when they did so much for me during our endless conversations, as they enthralled me with their wisdom and witty banter. I would have been happy to have pretend places at the table (for pretend friends) where everyone could be included. My mother never saw it that way, the realist that she had become.

My pretend friends' membership expanded and contracted, but Eugene and Apricot remained with me until the end. Maydris, another favorite with tenure, was embodied in my doll of the same name. My dear doll was at least half the size of my five-year-old self. I don't know exactly how to spell her name because it was never written, only murmured. I was barely learning to write when she was with me, and we all knew who we were.

I became the daughter of a dead daddy and a replacement. My mother walked around in her sweet and funny way with her heart ripped out of her dress and her eyes watching all the time for something to happen or someone to arrive. She married beautifully once and tragically later. She was still in her 20s for both marriages and, in this one, wore her war widowhood like the hat she often forgot to take off while she cooked dinner. We would rush home to prepare the scene for my new daddy's return from work. She'd count on me to remind her that she was still wearing her shopping or bridge club hat. She never wanted him to know we'd been away from the nest all day. The women of the 1950s kept a strange rulebook copied from a distant military code their post-war husbands imported from a former war life. It was some vain attempt to keep women subservient and obedient. The thing is there was that scarcity of safety everywhere, except with my pretend friends. I don't know how I knew that's what they were. Perhaps I heard my parents' concern about my vivid but unrealistic tendencies toward bizarre flights of imagination. These flights were deemed mostly inappropriate and indicative of a girl living in a dream world—my new daddy's lifelong assessment of me.

No one knew what to make of my "imagination," except my grandparents who found it and me perfectly charming. Everyone else spoke hopefully of a "phase." A phase was something highly regarded as a solution in the early 1950s for children who didn't fit well into the mold or who surprised parents with unexpected lapses in society-sanctioned behaviors. I was given to dreaminess and romantic ideas, but I eventually stopped receiving visits from my pretend friends, and my accents were corrected by a few visits to a speech pathologist. I gave everyone pause, though the obvious cause was never addressed because no one had words for it yet. As I left for school, my pretend friends remained at home with my behatted mother.

They managed to hang around the edges of my life until, maybe, third grade. By then, I was enjoying the periodic but dramatic appearances of a fully feathered and stunning Native American chief. He visited sometimes in my cold, narrow room in our house. This was in a part of upper Michigan few know and that sane people avoided in the winter. He was another kind of hero for me in those days, and we had many nice and cozy talks within the tented folds of my quilts. We could see our breath in there—it was so cold—and the windows were forever frosted over like it was Christmas Eve every night and day. Soon thereafter, hastened by my urge to grow up, get nylons, and watch television, they all evaporated—even Eugene and the exotic chief. I remember them now exactly as they were; and when I want to think about them, I can. I don't usually, but this is a special occasion.

REMARRIAGE AND DISLOCATION

My mother purposefully distanced herself from her interrupted life with my father by storing her grief in all the soft parts of her tiny body. Over time, it would tear through her from the inside out in lethal shards of grief, rage, and depression.

She remarried when I was almost three. Hal Ravely was an older handsome bachelor and former Army officer who had been wounded in the war. He thought his days in the US Army were the days of his glory, but he never spoke highly of them. He had a built-in resentment for fighter pilots, which would color their marriage in ways neither could imagine. Post-war society dictated that widows with children remarry in haste, but she told everyone that she truly loved her new beau who adopted me and became my "new daddy."

The story he told was that he was being ambivalent about marriage, but she had her sights set on him because he was an eligible catch. He had a steady job and was on his way to managing his own store. He said that she dressed me up in my best dress, shoes, hat, and gloves and brought me to his store one afternoon. I was, they said, prompted to ask him if he would be my daddy. He said he found me irresistible. As he would say, he married both of us.

The wedding was at Immaculate Conception Church, where Mother and I had been baptized. At the reception, held in my Aunt Virginia and Uncle Clark's house in an exclusive neighborhood of mansions, my mother looked happily into the camera. The suit she wore was the last expensive thing she ever bought for herself. In retrospect, she looked dangerously thin.

We moved to Minneapolis for my new daddy's job but not until after what I've been told was a "come to Jesus" meeting between my paternal grandparents and my mother's new husband. Ground rules were established along with visitation that would cut both ways and included a fair amount of displeasure at my departure. Simply put, my paternal grandparents didn't like or trust Hal. Of course, they wondered if it was because he had replaced their precious son, my father, their beloved daughter-in-law's husband, but there was more about Hal that made them uneasy.

Consequently, I would spend every summer and some holidays with my grandparents. I would have a few weeks in whatever town we were living in at the time with my school friends before I boarded a train and made my way to Cedar Rapids, Iowa, or Enid, Oklahoma. It was what I did and how I claim that my parents and my grandparents raised me in equal measure. I felt lucky indeed. My mother encouraged my escape back into the arms of my grandparents and never hesitated to grant me an extension if I wanted to stay longer.

"THANK YOU. MY DADDY DIED IN THE WAR."

The highlight of my week, as an only child in a new home, was garbage day. Against my mother's warnings, I would sit on the curb waiting for the big, stinky truck to turn the corner. I held my nose until the garbage men jumped off the truck to toss our trash from a single metal can into the maw of the truck. It was that maw that scared me, not the garbage men. They would always compliment me on my "pretty red hair," to which I would reply, "Thank you. My daddy died in the war." Those eight words, not counting my mannerly thank you, tell the story and define my difficult inheritance.

Clearly, I was a precocious child who felt different; but I had no idea, until many years later, exactly why or how that difference defined my life. I also believed I was the only girl whose father never came home from war.

My mother was pregnant three times after she remarried, but all three babies died before leaving the hospital. Roxanne, the only girl, lived five days. James Oliver and James Stewart had even shorter lives. My new daddy built a tiny casket each time and drove it to his family plot in St. Cloud, Minnesota. All I knew was that I wasn't going to have a new brother or sister any time soon.

Mother cried a little, listened to her records, and gazed into space with me on her lap. I would read to her from my picture books with the hope of bringing her back to me, but she was long lost to us both. My new daddy was determined to bring her firmly into what he called "reality." He didn't approve of my grandparents' influence on either of us, nor did he seek to understand her sorrow. I am certain that my mother was torn between old and new loyalties. It must have been inelegant and difficult for her, and it forced her into a secret relationship with my grandparents that never should have been necessary.

He took her to a psychiatrist when she became dark and depressed, telling the doctor he had no idea what was wrong with her. He often told the story that the doctor told her to "grow up." My new daddy took to calling her crazy, and she would argue in her own defense. I frequently found my small self in the midst of their fights. Not all were verbal.

When I was seven, and the three dead babies were the last attempt at pregnancy, we adopted my brother, Mark Alan. I chose his middle name based on a boy from my second grade class whom I found interesting. Mark was intended to be the son my father really wanted, as well as a safe way for them to have children. Their track record in combined DNA had been risky and painful.

Before my mother could receive the Catholic Church's considered blessing to use birth control, she had two more children: my sister, Christine and brother, Tom. Each would barely survive their traumatic births and suffered from the same disease as the first three. Medicine had improved the mortality of babies with lung disease, and though each had lingering effects from their traumatic births, they survived and thrived.

Thus, our growing family of six moved every year or two with our father's job. With each move, Mom adapted to ways of the life she was given. Our parents played bridge and golf, belonged to country clubs, and took us on long driving vacations, sometimes with trailers attached to the family station wagon. Of course, we were all smokers—our parents provided the smoke at home and in every car we owned. My responsibilities as second mother to my siblings involved watching them with a careful eye, playing with them, taking them outside to give our mother a rest, and evolving general maintenance. This entitles me to say that I've been raising children since I was seven.

Over time, Mother spoke nothing of her losses or the condition of her marriage. In 1962, when President and Jackie Kennedy's baby, Patrick, died of the same lung disease as her three children, she wrote them a condolence letter. She received a lovely, brief note from Mrs. Kennedy, which she treasured, even though she and daddy were staunch Republicans.

Grief ran through my mother's veins like spilled dark ink. She would tell it differently by reminding me, "Death is part of life and war." Though true, the woman my father loved died with him. The woman my second father married was whittled away by her new life and her own fragility. Despite her losses, she was mandated by her standards of solitary motherhood to shepherd me into adulthood. Sometimes, it was as if she suddenly remembered I was there. At other times, she was simply overwhelmed with the sheer force of what she was expected to accept. She urged me to learn how to cope as she did, which I did in my own way and in my own time.

A conspiracy of cancers claimed her when she was 59. Each of her adult children was allowed to see her once after she announced that she was dying. Only her sister Madge and our daddy were with her at the end. He told us that he saw her smile like the healthy young woman she once was as she spoke her last words: "Hi, honey. I've been waiting." Even he admitted that she was probably seeing her first husband again.

By that time, she'd buried both of her parents, three children, a suicidal brother, an alcoholic sister, and her own dreams. When my sister revealed the long-held family secret about our mother's three suicide attempts in the years after I'd left home, a subtle accusation was embedded in this truth: I had abandoned my siblings to our mother's demons and our father's violence. I knew only what our mother wanted me to believe, and she was masterful at shading the truth of her own suffering. As I created my own reality, it didn't include the darkness I left behind in which my siblings floundered. While it was stunning to envision my mother's death wish, it coincided with her inability to grieve her lost first husband, her three dead children, and her peace of mind. Grief and cancer are cantankerous allies.

At her funeral in Bull Shoals, Arkansas, where they retired, a minister we'd never met gave her eulogy. He barely knew her. His words were meaningless, empty platitudes. She'd long ago left her Catholicism behind, and he was the only clergy she knew and liked. None of her children were invited to speak about her; none volunteered. I barely listened, as I was doing my best to keep body and soul together while entertaining my baby niece, Mary—our sweet distraction.

There was no burial because our daddy didn't want one. He said he gave her ashes to the funeral home director and told him to dispose of them in whatever way he saw fit. All four of our mother's children were devastated and furious. He dismissed us and said that her body belonged to him. It was a grim day in Arkansas, and my siblings were inconsolable. He insisted that we go through her possessions and clothes and have everything out of the house so he wouldn't be reminded of her. Needless to say, we scrambled to accomplish this incomparable task, and much was lost in those moments of indecision and grief. I remember most vividly her slippers, still by her side of the bed. They looked as forlorn as we felt. To this day, I can't figure out what each of us took away except extreme sorrow and a paltry collection of memories.

Amidst the loss, I found resolution. I deeply grieved her but felt freed to consider what might have happened to my first father. It felt incomplete to accept the uncertainties of his absence. I became a self-appointed, fearless, truth-seeking daughter. It was what I could do when there was nothing to do but "accept it and move on." I decided to "move on" in another direction that had little to do with acceptance and everything to do with determination. I decided to fulfill the promise I made to my Nana at Woolworth's lunch counter: I would find my father and bring him home. When my adopted daddy died in 1991, I knew I could embark on this quest with no fear of doing harm to my parents' secret fears or resentments. Once I dared to tell him I was curious about my first father, and he reminded me that *he* was my father. I never dared to wonder aloud again . . . until 1991.

LETTERS LOST AND RECLAIMED

Once, all I knew of my father was contained in 450 letters written between 1941 and 1945. In some ways, they are also all I know of the woman who was my mother. The mother who raised me was another version of the woman my father called his "darling," his "guiding star," his "angel." I know about loving her as a mother and confidant, but I never knew the joyous woman who received these letters. They are proof positive that my father's life was wide, if not long. They tell me more about him than I have yet to learn about myself all these years later. While I am still wrestling with the mysteries of life, he accomplished all he came to do in 22 years.

I am the organizer and guardian of this remarkable correspondence, written (and illustrated) first by a teenage boy to his high school sweetheart and later by the man he became to his lover, wife, and friend. I became a voyeur, and his letters a window through which I peered, seeking insight and finding inspiration. They wrote a love story that is mine to tell.

Without these letters, I would have never known that my handwriting is identical to my father's, the names of the books he read, the music he preferred, his feelings about dying in combat, about parenthood, about sex and yearning, about social injustice, and what it was like to go to war in 1943.

They paint a clear, bittersweet picture of a man who loved a woman, his family, his country, his God, his life, and his baby daughter. Feelings are fine threads woven among words and then sewn into intricate, fragile designs. Their patterns, tangible and precious, are stitched together with my mother's mostly unseen letters.

War preempted ordinary life plans for the teenagers who were to become my parents. If a timeline were created from these letters, it would show my father's amazing, swift passage into adulthood, then into a hero's war. It would show my mother's own metamorphosis, hastened by a world in crisis and in response to the man she loved.

They bid their youth farewell to live out their brief, earthly relationship through correspondence. In reality, they spent very little physical time together—a few months in five years.

These letters are intimate and private. As compelling as I found them—and as endlessly fascinating as they were because the writers were my parents—I wondered if anyone else would care. Until I created a memorial video about my father, I didn't realize this story told in the film was universal and captivating. Fifty years later, my parents' 1940s love story resonated in a very different era.

My parents and countless other couples were separated by war in the 1940s. Letters were all that bound them in a time when telephone communication to and from war-torn countries was not an option. This was their marriage, their primary communication, their whispers in the dark, and their laughter in the sunlight. They never had a chance to become complacent, though my father writes of yearning for that possibility.

Their letters define their world, making it possible to read beyond the words, to savor their unwavering honesty and commitment, and to appreciate the courage it takes to go to war. My father maintained an undiminished love for his country, a passion about flying, and an allegiance to his squadron mates. By reading them, it became possible for me to know the man who was my father and wonder how his voice sounded.

Because of his letters, I know my father. I know how well he loved my mother and me and that he believed he would return home to us after the war. My grandmother's cautionary warning against papering over my history, as my mother had, was heeded—though not without her skill and mine. Thus, I include excerpts of the letters to include my father, with whom I have enjoined on this quest.

1940, Franklin High School, Cedar Rapids, Iowa

Honey: During Art this morning I got to thinking about you and could hardly bring myself to realize that I had found you. That may sound kinda queer, but it's the way I feel. Kind of like a little kid when he gets a swell new bike or something. For a while he's mighty happy about it, of course, but he doesn't realize how much he appreciates it sometimes until a time has passed. Maybe some evening he'll be lying in bed just thinking and it will occur to him that he really he [emphasis his] has that swell bike that is the envy of the neighborhood and he is overcome by joy. That's just the way I felt in Art this morning when I was thinking about you. Seeing you after class topped it off beautifully. I fell in love all over again. All my love, Skinny P.S. Honey, I love you, SEE?

Sweetheart: Irrespective of the fact that the grim shadow of religion class hangs not ten minutes away, I shall write you. From here on in this letter, I shall review all I have said—I love you with all of my heart and soul, so much that I would die for you, darling. You know full well that I wouldn't do one thing to hurt you in any way honey, even in the slightest. Your merest wish, and I say this in all seriousness, is my command. So please, if I do anything that you dislike even in the slightest, please, dearest, tell me, and a solid attempt will be made to rectify whatever it is. See, honey?

The bell should ring any minute now so this may be cut rather short, but this writing to you is the second best to being with you, with the exception, of course, of the medium of my friendly enemy, the telephone, which in my estimation, is fine for ordering doughnuts and fresh fish. This teacher certainly is having a great time trying to see what I'm doing but she's too lazy to come back and investigate. All my love. Skinny.

My parents' letters before and during WWII came to me much later than 1941 and far beyond Cedar Rapids, Iowa, where my parents met and courted. During one of my adult Enid visits, Nana Lettie emerged from the basement with what would forever give me purposeful direction. Inspiration and motivation were tied with faded green ribbons, rescued and stored in a silver strongbox that held my parents' long-lost correspondence along with a soft, black scrapbook. My Nana had quietly reclaimed each piece as it flew away from my mother's grieving heart. Without my mother's approval, I am certain, Nana presented me with the things my father wore, touched, read, created, or wrote. I sensed her reverence and accepted them from her, knowing I was receiving pieces of a puzzle I might never solve and with little idea of the picture I was trying to assemble. Everything collected fit together only as a murky, long-abandoned mystery. What remained certain was that WWII, like all other wars, carried the seduction of patriotic duty, cloaked in the certainty of collective desperation, political greed, and anger, and fueled by the lurking possibility of heroism.

It was a medium-sized, silver metal box, heavy with letters. With a sigh of certainty, Nana Lettie handed me the one thing that would alter my consciousness beyond scarlet fever and any previous adjustment to the madness of my life. How did she know I wouldn't use them in a decoupage project or dump them for the nice silver box? I was barely a shadow of my current self in depth or scope. I was a young mother by then, and though I held a large part of me in reserve as the daughter who loved her dead father, I had another quite-alive set of parents who had raised me to abandon or, at least, repress my wandering imagination and visits with the dead. I was turned around like a runaway train with all engines running and pouring steam whenever I'd venture back in time. "Be realistic. Get your head outta the clouds." Now, all resolution dissolved as I received the letters packed with courage and tied with green ribbons.

I took them home and added them to my list of things I would save in case of fire: Two baby daughters topped all my lists; then my black, formerly musical lamb given to me at birth and the only surviving witness to the pretend friends era; a silver bracelet with *Sherrie* engraved across the bar; and all my picture albums, including the scrapbook my mother and father kept during the war. He would send her things to save, which she would carefully paste onto the black pages and identify in white ink. It was a tattered mess by the time I received it, but it was a treasured part of the puzzle I would spend the next four decades reassembling.

Some time around the letters and strongbox gifting, my grandmother also gave me two of my father's uniform jackets. He was an impeccable and precise dresser—mindful of style, color, function, and fabric. He had *all* of his clothes tailored, including his military uniforms. In later letters, he would complain about the absence of dry cleaners and the availability of laundry and pressing facilities on the flight line. He hated being dirty and wrinkled. These two uniform jackets proved that. They are preserved now in two museums.

When my mother visited the next time, I held up the jackets and said, "Nana gave me my father's uniform jackets." My mother transformed instantly from the nearly 50-year-old woman she was into a much younger, lighter, and, perhaps, former version of herself. She never took the jackets from me, but stroked them from shoulder to front pocket in a way that caught my breath. She ran her hand down the front of each jacket, patted them, and walked away. It was one of the most intimate things I had ever witnessed.

Did she see him in them? Should I have known? How was it for her to have this irrefutable evidence of his existence suddenly appear? She had a wistful and lost smile, a half attempt at remembering, and then the certain closing of that door, as if someone was telling her she could never return unless she walked away now. She lived less than a decade after that, but only in part because of the empty jackets. Smoking all her life took her from me. In my father's letters, he would say only bad things about smoking as it related to his choices in the matter. I sensed that she smoked then, and he didn't approve, but he wasn't a disapproving or shaming kind of guy. He probably figured he'd deal with that in his loving way after the war. Instead, when she remarried, she smoked herself to death. She died just short of her sixtieth birthday, and my only comfort is that she is with my father.

I, on the other hand, remained an unfinished story. He was my father for three actual weeks plus the nine months when my mother was pregnant with me. They didn't guess right about me being a girl, but it was clear that they loved me anyway. It was pretty swell having all that love in the bank even before the stork dropped me in Cedar Rapids, Iowa, in March of 1945, right into the eager and cozy arms of my father's parents. This was a time when new mothers were expected to rest at least nine days while other, more qualified people tended to the baby. While my mother languished in that arrangement, my grandparents (the self-appointed attendants to the precious heiress) maintained a constant presence at the nursery window, which led to an early dismissal of my mother and me from Mercy Hospital. This was exactly my grandparents' fondest wish—to be alone with their granddaughter. My grandparents always got their way and loved each other even more than they loved their own children and me.

Their one irretrievable loss (except each other to death much later in their story) was their beloved eldest son. Imagine how their love for me flowed exponentially, covering everything, sealing all the possible holes of my existence, as they gathered their dead son's memory into their hearts for safe keeping and sharing with me as I grew. They did that and more and forevermore managed to keep him present in my life.

I don't know for sure, but the final letters that passed between my parents during the first weeks of my life were probably on a two-week time delay that the postal department offered during wartime. Since my father lived his last weeks in the three that followed my birth, communication was crucial. As I read the letters from my father and some from my mother during those fleeting new-baby weeks, life was about feeding me, changing my pants, handing me back and forth between my ever-present grandparents and maternal Nana, buying me things, and spending mindless hours just gazing upon my baby-spitting and crying countenance for clues of family resemblance. They thought I looked exactly like my father, and everything about me reminded them of him. My mother loved best the emerging wisps of red hair that made my paternity certain, as if it were not.

During the 1992 summer before I started graduate school, I began transcribing my parents' letters. Knowing that I needed to preserve them against time, transcription was the first step toward that end. By then, all three of my parents were dead, and I felt bold enough to draw back the curtain of my birthparents' intimate legacy. I was free to know them through the lens of their own writing. I planned to finish by the end of the summer, fearing that the demands of graduate school would preclude my ability and interest in such a project.

How could I know that the letters would engender the research I would do in two graduate programs? A bigger picture emerged as I wondered about the lived experience (mine and others) of father-loss in war. Of the 78,000 missing or killed in action, some had children.

INVOKING
PERMISSION

B efore I transcribed the first syllable of the first word of the first letter, I asked my parents to grant me their permission to complete this tender project or to help me sabotage it with a swift kick of boredom and procrastination. Their blessing flowed immediately and melodically from their letters to my typing fingers onto thousands of pages. Five enormous binders, one for each section of my parents' lives together and apart, were filled and labeled by years and months: 1941 and 1942; 1943 February, March, April; 1943 May to December; 1944 January to December; 1945 January to April; and Mary Kathryn Taylor Estill's Last Letters, an undated section for my mother's heartbreaking letters written to her dead husband. These were her desperate testimony to "make it not true" by undoing the truth, acting as if she had never received a telegram saying her husband was missing in action.

My parents emerged from their letters like holograms. They led me back to the early 1940s of their courtship and informed my life in ways family anecdotes never could. I saw them as high school sweethearts whose 1941 graduation year coincided with the events at Pearl Harbor, thrusting the nation into war. My father was determined to enlist but had to wait months to be inducted. He would visit the recruiting office every week as they continued to place all the young men who came forward after Pearl Harbor. He went to work in the interim but wrote often of his frustration that he wasn't yet tapped to go to basic training.

4/13/1942

Darlin': It was nice to talk to you today—I only wish that I could have come to Cedar Rapids, but we just finished working, so my making the trip would be well nigh impossible. About the army scare that you gals seem to have contracted, I went over to Rock Island Wednesday noon to enlist in the Air Corps. "Of course," the recruiting officer informed me, "the only ones who can sign you are the officers of the traveling examination board, which will be through in May." Upon further questioning, he disclosed that I might write to Corps Area Headquarters at Chicago and obtain permission to come and take the examination. So, a friend of Milo's, who, incidentally, is a Senator, has offered to write a letter asking that I be given an audience. Meanwhile, I've written the Commander of the Canadian Air Force, inquiring after details of requirements for enlistment in that Air Force. The two are fighting side by side all over the world, so that would be o.k.

If I fail to succeed in both of these attempts, I'm going to join the Marine Corps and try to get into the Commandos after my five weeks training period. Those boys really see the results of their work. Their only arms are a 25-caliber pistol and a six-inch knife, plus hand grenade. They are the ones who sneak into the enemy harbors, kill a sentry or two, and make off with a kidnapped enemy officer. Almost every day, the newspapers carry stories concerning the deeds of the British Commandos in Norway.

Please, honey, realize this: I shall inform you of each and every new development. Tonite during my dinner hour, I visited the barbershop and fell asleep in the chair. . . . This is about all for now, honey. Be a good little girl, and I'll bring you a present. Love and XXXXX's, Gener

Tension was high among those waiting to be called to duty. Unimaginably, their idyllic, tidy lives would be upended in such a short time. Still, everything was magnified, and those who were in love, or thinking about being in love, accelerated things by getting engaged or married. There was an urgency to create one thing that would be sustaining and hopeful for the future. My parents became engaged with a tiny diamond ring and lovers' spats:

1/10/1944

Dearest: Certainly you remember the night you thought we'd lost your ring? If memory serves, we were at the Yacht Club, and while you were telling me goodbye forever, the ring came off your finger and was placed on the table. "Ah, this is the chance I've been waiting for! I've warned her again and again that she'll lose the bloomin' thing if she persists in removing it whenever we have a difference," I thought. Thereupon, I surreptitiously placed the ring—for the present forgotten by you—on the auto key chain. Soon thereafter, we entered the car and drove down Ellis Blvd. A few moments passed, and you asked if I had the ring. "Why, didn't you pick it up?" was my horrified rejoinder. "Anyway, you apparently didn't care much about it." Finally, you prevailed upon me to return to inquire concerning the ring. If you'll recall, I went in alone and returned shortly. Quite naturally, you were led to believe that someone had made off with it.

Such moans and wailing!!! Great tears welled into your pretty eyes. (Here's where I begin to weaken.) Your lower lip would have made a suitable perch for a rooster that nite. How you condemned yourself for such gross neglect. If you ever found your little ring, you'd never take it off again, you swore. Against such tearful eloquence I could not prevail. Even my heart of stone melted at your sobs. So, I proudly held up the key chain, with the ring affixed, to assure you it was safe.

Honey, sometimes I wonder if we weren't both nutz. All of it was such fun, tho', and there are so many wonderful memories. I simply cannot imagine how I'd have gotten along if we hadn't met. Somehow, you are, and seem to always have been, just what makes my happiness complete.

Their correspondence, begun at Franklin High School in Cedar Rapids, Iowa, wove its way through his first and only civilian job after graduation—at John Deere Farm Implement Company in Waterloo, Iowa—around the airfields and barracks of his basic and advanced flight training in Texas, Arizona, and California, and through his days and nights as a flight instructor.

I learned there is a finite amount of information contained in 450 letters; 3,000 sheets of airmail paper, v-mails, envelopes, small articles, and illustrations. These treasures included medals with precise lettering and meaning: one, a heart, fired all over with royal purple enamel; a tie bar embellished with a bucking bronco on leather; a scrapbook in dire need of revision and reclamation; a small collection of original drawings that included a colored pencil sketch of de Gaulle, Churchill, and Eisenhower, and a sweet self-portrait of my father as a teenager.

His parents received notice from the War Department Air Corps from a Major General of the US Army—a form letter, though it was typed and signed personally by the major general. In those days, parents were proud to be sending their sons to war, and the War Department expected nothing less.

2 /16/1943

Sweetheart: At last! I was classified today—from the looks of the letter from headquarters, I was eligible for all three types of training, but according to my choice, I was classified pilot.

I watched them fall in love. I witnessed them nervously plan their simple wedding in Fort Stockton, Texas, near my father's first flight training airbase; they invited my mother's sister, Madge Taylor, and my father's closest friend, Jack Downer, to witness their marriage. My Aunt Madge was my mother's best friend; my father and Jack, friends since high school, had been through flight training together.

I noticed how my father's writing took on a more intimate tone after their wedding night. They were married on his birthday, June 26, after which she returned home to Cedar Rapids.

6/29/1943

Dear one: One of the boys asked me if I'd gone to sleep last nite. Said that my eyes looked black and blue around the lids. Couldn't tell him that I lay awake all nite worrying about birth control. (I'm only kiddin' sweetie.) (You are my sweetie, aren't you?)

The rhythm of my parents' relationship was indelibly etched in these letters. Rather than intruding, I felt invited. I knew my parents had dearly loved me. It was easy for me to step, at last, into my place as their daughter. He wrote a treatise on marriage from the front lines in Europe:

11/25/1944

Precious one: I'm afraid that a report of my day's activities would not include more than constant thoughts and memories of you. Of the sweet, fresh, precious you of our high school days, the adorable wonderful you of our marriage. Honestly, darlin', I do get such a kick out of you, simply remembering the things you've done, things you've said, and especially your wonderful reactions to my various and assorted hair-brained ideas. You've been a gloriously precious wife, my dear, and I'm so proud and wildly happy to be your husband.

We can quite naturally view with amusement the various fights and scraps we've had, but I shudder to imagine my fate had you fulfilled your threats of casting me out of your heart. And yet how I thrill that you failed, through the goodness of your dear heart, to accomplish that dreaded mission. What a wonderful, wonderful wife you are, my dear. Do suppose my ravings sound rather strange, but that is precisely the tenor of my thoughts. Never dreamed that one could be so far, yet seem so near as you sometimes do.

She managed to visit him before he went overseas and as he completed his final phase of flight training at Hamilton Air Base in Santa Rosa, California. They met for the last time at one of the old hotels in San Francisco, where they were given a luxury suite because we were a grateful nation. My mother told me their parting gift that weekend was me!

She arrived at the hotel and was told that her husband was delayed. Their two-level suite had a dramatic staircase in the middle, or at least it was made dramatic by what happened. Expecting to be alone, she was surprised to hear my father's voice from the top of the stairs. She looked up to see her husband wearing only his officer's cap. It sailed down the stairs to land at her feet. There is no wonder how I came into the world as a romantic child.

When my father learned of my mother's pregnancy with me, he also learned that his mother dreamed that the baby would be a boy. From then on, I was called "Mike," and his letters included whimsical advice for my mother:

12/14/1944

As soon as the baby arrives, you'd best arrange a carrier similar to that employed by Indian mothers. On this basket, install a transparent turret, similar to those found on bombers. From such an advantageous position, the baby will be able to spot all pickpockets. Of course, some sort of intercom system will have to be developed. The baby will always wear a throat mic and you a headset. OK—you're all set up—this will be a typical message from the baby: "Check this blonde coming in from 9:00, Woo Woo!!" (Well, she wasn't a pickpocket, but the kid is evidently enjoying his work.) You'll be a slight bit more conspicuous than the average shopper, but the complete freedom from worry more than compensates for that little inconvenience.

12/30/1944

Of late you've been so positive Mike will be a boy. What if, by some quirk of nature, he's a little girl? Lil' girls aren't out of season, you know, honey, and what a cute one she'd be!!! I can hardly wait to see our baby, baby.

1/11/1945

Every day brings the baby closer, honey. Gee, you're smart, knowing how to get the little rascals. I NEVER would have thought of that!

When I lived in San Francisco 24 years later, I would walk past that old, elegant hotel and think of my parents at my age loving each other enough to make every moment of the few they had together precious and permanent.

He wrote to her while living with his squadron in the Château le Beauchêne near the village of Falaën, Belgium, and from tents on a muddy spring airfield in Euskirchen, Germany.

1/17/1945, Belgium

Howdy, honey: Little kids never fail to amaze me. Yesterday, dozing over a book, I imagined I heard the voices of children, but paid no heed. The clamor grew insistently louder, however, and I finally went to the window to investigate. There, in the snow below, stood a simply tremendous Belgian workhorse. He must have been 18 to 20 hands high and very powerfully muscled; a veritable mountain of horseflesh, all harnessed and strapped. Attached to the harness bar were six tiny sleds in trail, each bearing a child. The eldest of the troop was, at the most, seven or eight years, while the youngest couldn't have been over three or so. The infant on the lead sled had the reins in her hands and was ordering that monstrous beast around as tho' he were a puppy.

The great front lawn of the chateau was covered with fresh snow, so out they went. The group cavorted and played for almost a half hour in the new snow, frequently stopping to dismount from their sleds and investigate some new curiosity in the woods. The horse seemed to realize that he was more or less responsible for the babies, because he refused to move while they were playing around his feet. Finally, tiring of this playground, the happy bunch trouped off down the lane from whence they'd come. Watching those little tykes, one finds it difficult to believe they have had war so near, perhaps even lost some of their families or playmates to it. Just seeing these little kids over here is reason enough to make it a positive pleasure to work over Adolph's boys.

DEATH-
ANNOUNCING
TELEGRAMS

For the family of an active duty service member, military bereavement starts with a knock at the door. The news comes in person, by a military chaplain and a service member whose rank is equal to or higher than that of the one who has died. They arrive in full-dress uniform, bearing the worst news possible. It's the visit no family wants.

American families who lost a loved one generally hid their suffering. With the arrival of the death-announcing telegram, silence descended like a fog. As children, we absorbed the grief that enveloped our families, silence that obscured knowledge of our fathers and often negated awareness that we, as children, were affected by our fathers' deaths. Silence characterizes the war orphans' experiences and intensified their loss. (Lost in the Victory, *Hadler and Mix, xix)*

On April 30, 1945, at 6:59 p.m., my mother received the first telegram declaring her husband missing in action on Friday,

April 13, 1945. She told me she dropped the telegram, picked up her purse, and headed out the door to kill herself. As she stood at the top of the stairs that led to her mother's apartment, she heard me crying in my crib. She decided not to leave me, but I will always believe the woman who received that telegram wanted to be missing too. She came back into the apartment, put down her purse, changed my diaper, and eventually wrote her husband a letter imploring him to return.

5/1/1945

Darling: Regardless of how things are, I've just got to write down what is going through my mind. I can't mail it now but later when things are better and I can send it to you. I want you to know everything that goes on just as I've always written. Yes, I got the blasted telegram last night. I can't say I expected it, but for the past week or so, something inside kept at me, and I just couldn't shake it. When I didn't have any mail yesterday, I guess I sorta had a hunch something was up. I'm keeping myself well in hand for both yours and Sherrie's sake. Sherrie feels everything I do, so I have to be careful I don't keep her all upset. I've never realized what a help she was going to be. You see, I've got you in her. I'm so glad you know about her, honey; that makes it so much better. I talked with Sister Carmel. She is so sweet, and she seemed to know just what to say to help me feel better. I guess this is certainly a strange letter, but that's how I am feeling. Tonight you made the front page; I'm only sorry it had to take this to do it. The paper notified everyone of the news, so, of course, we've been well supplied with visitors. Everyone thinks I'm strange because I don't sit with a tear-stained hankie and a lost look on my face. Honey, why I don't is beyond me—call it hope if you like, but I'll be darned if I know how or why I feel the way I do. I know deep in my heart you are alright, so I can afford to be patient. Heaven knows I love you with all my heart but I can't quite get myself to think you're not alright. Good night, my darling.

Six months later, on October 24, 1945, at 3:11 p.m., a second telegram arrived, indistinguishable from the first except for the words "killed in action." My father's status was amended, even though what happened after his plane went missing six months earlier was unknown. Believing he was arbitrarily declared dead, my mother returned my father's medals to the War Department in Washington, DC, along with a letter to the quartermaster general of the Army Service Forces:

Dear Sirs:

While I appreciate your response to my inquiries regarding my husband, much remains unclear. If my husband had been listed as missing for the full year period, I should understand why there were no details of his death or a grave. The fact that he was only missing six months, then declared dead, led us to believe that conclusive proof of death had been found. Even if there isn't a grave, there must have been something to bring about the declaration. I have decided to return, under separate cover, all the medals awarded my husband and recently received. I would prefer having information about my husband rather than awards you send me in an effort to rationalize his absence. Sincerely yours, Mrs. Shannon Eugene Estill

After the first telegram, she continued her daily writing practice. All sealed envelopes were addressed to my father's most recent APO box but never mailed. They remained unopened until I dared to violate those seals, finding them full of my mother's hopeful DNA and prayerful wishes. Each was written on personalized, shell pink airmail paper. Some had been returned and stamped "casualty mail or missing in action" in violent purple or red ink. Among the letters returned was one written close to the date he was killed where she refers to herself as "the cow," probably due to breastfeeding and everything else involved with caring for a newborn:

(Written by "The Cow." I don't know what a date is yet, but I am about 700 dirty diapers old.)

Dear Pop,

Just thought I'd better let you know how I'm getting along. First of all, I must say I think it's all right for Mommie to write to you every day, but does she have to write such long letters when I lay here all that time in wet pants?

You see, our nails are real long, and I have such fun picking my targets to scratch. What does Mommie do but tie up the ends of my sleeves with ribbons. Isn't there something you can do about that?

The nice thing around here is the cow they keep for me. They bring it in about every three hours and let me tank up. They used to bring it in the middle of the night, right in the middle of a wonderful dream about Van Johnson, but I fixed that. I pretended I was asleep, and now they leave me alone.

Sure have got my Nanas whipped into line in short order, if I do say so myself. It's quite good sport to lay here and make like I've got colic or something and watch them argue over the best way to help me. Those are the times Mommie says I'm just like you. What does "snarky look" mean?

You should see them dress me up and then have hysterics. What do they expect for three weeks, Lana Turner? I can always get even with them for such treatment by merely opening my mouth and letting my lungs do the rest. Another good trick is just not to burp. Mommie gets worried when I go to sleep right away without burping. So, when she lays me down and gets herself nicely asleep, I wake up with a gas pain. Clever girl that I am. I miss her when she's asleep.

Well, I guess I don't have anything else to discuss with you at the moment. I sure am anxious for you to come home, as I have a few little things in mind to try out on you!

Your loving, if slightly spoiled, daughter,

Sharon

P.S. Write me sometime. Mommie isn't very good about letting me read her mail.

After the second telegram, she stopped writing and surrendered her fragile hope that he would ever return to us. In a simple act of paradoxical injustice, everyone accepted my father's death without ever knowing if, how, or where he died. The war had ended six months earlier. In a final gesture of grief and despair, my mother discarded my father's letters. The entirety of my parents' relationship, including a sweet, young courtship, marriage, war, and a baby daughter, spanned less than a decade. He was 22 when he died, and she was barely 23.

The eventual divide between what would become East and West Germany with the construction of the Berlin Wall restricted travel in or out of East Germany for decades thereafter. US government investigative teams searching for missing pilots were denied entry even after the surrender in 1945. My father became one of thousands of American soldiers, marines, sailors, and pilots abandoned beyond closed borders.

12/26/1944

Hi Chub: This is absolutely a beautiful, breathtaking, awe-inspiring nite. Such moonlite perfection I've not seen for a long time. Somehow, it reminds me of an Iowa winter's nite, so cold and clear. The most amazing and thrilling thought of all is that the selfsame moon is shining down on you. I suppose you're howling about it. Tsk! Tsk! And in your condition. What are our chances on twins? Aw, c'mon honey, be a sport. Incidentally, does Dr. Day charge a flat rate or make a separate charge for each call? It seems that you once mentioned that it was a flat rate, not a piecework deal. Gloriously, another payday draws nigh. Will get a money order off as soon as possible after the great day. In *the same department, perhaps you'll recall my mentioning how little money I spend here. To date, I've spent approximately $17 in Dec., including all expenses, laundry, PX, rations, except the $21 food ration charge which is deducted from my salary. Good, huh? You no doubt wondered at the condition of the envelope I used for this note. Frankly, I've carried it about with me for nearly a week, searching for some mucilage for the flap. Today, no less than a miracle occurred. Collins and Griese, the two sackrats, emerged from their lethargy sufficiently to fell a tree and cut it up for firewood. It was truly an amazing spectacle because they are notorious for their lack of ambition. Being a paragon of industriousness myself, I can't quite understand why anyone should have an aversion to good old manual labor occasionally. (You recall how I loved each and every PT session.) Zounds! I see that the hour of midnite draws nigh!! So, to bed I go, my love, Gener. Honey, try to keep me in mind when you're thinking thoughts of love and kisses and stuff. Tell the baby hello. P.S. Am enclosing your birthday present in this letter. Gum is worth its weight in gold there, isn't it?*

Once I thought that simply publishing my parents' wartime letters would serve my purpose. After all, wasn't their love story indicative of 1940s America in its innocence and passion? Though my parents' letters were sweet and profound, there was much untold. The ending wouldn't be written until I wrote it. I couldn't write it until I figured out how their story ended.

I first read my parents' letters as a young mother seeking to gain advice (in absentia) from my father. I wondered if I was getting it right or if I was doing irreparable harm to my children by not reading the handbook on parenting. His unintentional wisdom brought me comfort and taught me about the man who was my father. Even more profoundly, it brought my mother into focus as a woman who sublimated her grief and, in the process, became another person. Here's my favorite letter:

Easter Sunday, 1945

Dearest Angels: I simply can't express how I feel at our daughter: so happy and glad, yet almost afraid. Afraid that I won't measure up to the shadowy indeterminate standards of parenthood. How I should love to be with you two now. Just can't understand how old Estill happened to land the two cutest gals in the world, but won't argue. Am afraid the Big Chief might check the records and discover that you really don't belong to me at all, but perhaps are angels that have sneaked down from heaven to tease this poor mortal.

It's those "shadowy indeterminate standards of parenthood" that I hoped I got right at least some of the time.

POST-WAR US: TWO NANAS AND A BANKA

Not everyone celebrated at the end of the war. Despite ticker tape parades in large cities, most of the men who survived drifted home without fanfare. Although many were badly damaged by their experiences, they received no counseling and rarely talked about what happened. They and their families were relieved the war was over and they were safe at home again. (Lost in the Victory, Hadler and Mix, xxi)

My mother continued working as a medical secretary with plans for nursing school after the war. I was happily grandparented by my two nanas and my grandfather, whom I called Banka. The family adults guessed that Banka's habit of giving me his silver change and sometimes his "green" money was the source of his name. Since Banka was one of my first words, it's unlikely that I knew enough about deposits and withdrawals to be that clever.

Nevertheless, my father's younger sister, Margie, the former favorite girl, resented the green money gifts given to me, as she had 19-year-old needs of her own. I would sit at her dressing table and touch all her bottles and brushes and puffs and powders. Those must have been the things she wanted to buy with my money. I'd sit there when she was out on a date or asleep. Both occurred frequently.

No one ever scolded me, including Aunt Margie, but everyone gave me loving boundaries about things like touching bees, sitting near the street on the curb, and eating unpeeled apples. Later, they added cutting out paper dolls or using scissors of any kind during a thunderstorm. Apparently, I was made of sugar, or so I was told.

I loved being with my two Nanas and my Banka. They lived at either end of B Avenue Northeast in Cedar Rapids, Iowa, and I learned to walk on the sidewalk between their houses. I can see my fancy Nana Nell behind me and my less fancy—but practical and loving—Nana Lettie in the distance. She wore house dresses; my Nana Nell wore heels, a corset, designer clothes, and big jewelry. Every morning, she sat in her small, cherry rocking chair by the window and "did her face." She would smoke a cigarette, shave her eyebrows so she could pencil in a more pleasing shape, and tell me that she hoped I would be pretty one day.

Nana Nell was rightfully concerned about my freckles and feckless hair. She was in the fashion business and worked at W. E. Cramer Department Store. She also modeled in New York and brought me bountiful gifts of Kate Greenaway dresses with pinafores and a stuffed giraffe that was just my size from the flagship FAO Schwarz toy store.

When I outgrew magnificent toy store gifts, she brought me a Poor Pitiful Pearl doll. She was, in a word, pitiful. Saggy socks, dirty face, untidy dress, scuffed shoes—about like me. I loved her. Nana said it was the last doll I'd ever need or want. She was partly right.

A few years ago, I returned to B Avenue Northeast and made a ceremonial walk between my Nanas' houses. I could see them, one launching, one waiting for me to land. It was the same street where I would stand below Nana Nell's second-floor apartment screened porch as she watched me perform all the dance routines I had learned since my last visit. A favorite, which I taught my best friend, Jeannie Willenborg, who lived next door in Cedar Rapids, was a song and dance number that involved swaying like a lilac tree. I've never seen a lilac tree sway, as all the lilacs I've seen seem to grow on bushes; but there we were, swaying back and forth, heartily singing the song my dance teacher taught me: "Lilac tree, lilac tree, bending and swaying." Nana Nell would applaud from the porch along with my Uncle Jack, who lived with her. He would read the paper during these shows. The two of them would sit in their private box, drinking beer, smoking cigarettes, and playing cribbage while the show went on. Their porch routine never varied, even if it was early in the morning, noon, or night.

I learned to play very competitive jacks on that sidewalk, and I was allowed to ride my little purple tricycle as far as the corner but never out of sight. I was happily oblivious to my entertainment value, as I took it all seriously and with great joy. At my Nana Nell's insistence, I was well dressed, even for riding my trike in the neighborhood.

Jeannie Willenborg and her brother Johnnie attended my first birthday, or so I've been told. Johnnie, finding me less adorable than the rest of the world, pushed my face in my cake. He denied it later, but somewhere there is a picture of a shocked, cake-faced little girl. He collected baseball cards and would teach us the names of the famous players of the day. I still remember some of them as their deaths are mourned in modern times.

Jeanne and I remained summer friends through high school. I received my first kiss the summer we were boy crazy together—just before seventh grade. The boy was called Doug Brimmer from Marshalltown, Iowa. After a blessedly brief kiss, I was embarrassed. I patted his shoulder as I got up from the step in front of my Nana and Banka's house where it happened and went inside. I never forgot the moment or the surprised boy who picked up his bike and rode home.

My Banka was a dedicated letter writer, evidenced by the frequent, terse demands directed toward the War Department. He expected the government to find his son and provide the family the answers they needed to put him to rest or bring him home. The unknown, the fantasy, and the possibilities haunted my grandparents and my father's siblings for as long as they lived.

Perhaps my father's taste in tailoring and fine clothing began at a young age. Toward the end of his life, he reminded my mother of his upbringing and ability to make light of what was probably a fine obsession with haberdashery:

As a civilian, once upon a time, my dress was always correct. As witness, the yellow scarf and gloves with saddle shoes and the short raincoat. What could have been more appropriate for evening wear?

Nana Lettie and Banka Estill lived in two places: Cedar Rapids, Iowa, and Enid, Oklahoma, which seemed normal to me. I had a sweet Wedgwood-blue back bedroom in the Enid house that Nana's father built for her as a wedding present. His signature is still visible on the foundation.

Nana Lettie wasn't glamorous, but she ran a comfy house full of love while managing the oil fields and wheat farms left to her by her parents and grandparents. I loved being there because my foundation was rooted beneath that house where my father was raised. It still stands, somewhat disheveled and unloved but nonetheless the container for my most cherished childhood memories.

AN UNDERSTORY AND A PUZZLEMENT

arranging
rearranging
fixing
unfixing
boxing
unboxing
the present
the past
finding
losing
the pendulum swings
across my chest
lower each time

Christine Jensen Hogan
Daughter of Al Jensen, KIA March 1945

I felt then, as I do now, that curiosity about father-loss in war is my birthright, enhanced by tender stories and reverent silences. It grew over time with the accumulation of interest fueled by passion and lived within me, awaiting the day I would transform it into something tangible and explanatory. Thus, a father-quest became a culmination of years, tears, hopes, determination, and a pursuit of the unknown.

I relate so well to Christine Jensen Hogan's poem. Even as I eventually found myself "boxing and unboxing" materials that connected me to my father-story, I had no idea what purpose they would ever serve except as sentimental reminders of what could have been. Along the way, my interest expanded from "the past" to "the present." I wondered about other women who, like me, had experienced "losing" their father in war and "finding" him in similar collections and stories.

When I chose my doctoral dissertation research topic in 2000, I intended to explore this loss in a detached but scholarly way. I wanted to get beneath the experience I knew so little yet so much about. If I approached it intellectually, not emotionally, the answers might present themselves in a way I could manage. Despite that fail-safe method, I suspected that what I would discover would take the lid off whatever caused so much sadness and yearning.

Outside of psychology texts, would there be interest in little girls, now women, who still missed their daddies? All I knew was that it was becoming increasingly apparent that this loss seemed to seriously influence my life choices. The exploration began with what humanistic psychologist Clark Moustakas (1990) calls the "puzzlement" about discovering others who responded as I did to this loss and who similarly yearned for connection. I began "arranging" and "rearranging" the notion that I could contribute to a mostly unexplored body of knowledge. I learned that at least 200,000 American children's fathers died in WWII. Were there others, like me, who were curious to learn more about how we fared as a result of our unique and unexplored early childhood father-loss?

Though my parents' WWII letters were never published in their entirety as a love story, they continue to guide me. By looking at the puzzlement, I honor my parents who aren't here to see what I have created from the deep crater my father's death left in our lives. It was not an irretrievable loss after all, but an opportunity to create new reality from an old truth.

The rhythms I found on the quest have become synchronistic. I have had the privilege of sequestering myself on a blue houseboat and traveling the world, carrying only my curiosity, in order to make sense of the question. There were times when I felt eccentric and self-absorbed, but never alone or without possibility.

My conclusions are drawn from the earth and a once-upon-a-time beginning. At first, history blocked my passage within the vagaries and confusions of impenetrable war. Imaginings of my lost father didn't hold me there with him, nor did I want to be mired in the past. Instead, this quest for elegy and truth gave me purpose in reflection and the realization that my loyalty and love have kept me tethered to this story. For those of us whose fathers die in war, our wings are clipped. Through this exploration, mine have been reconstituted and are even more luscious and feathered.

In return, I am able to fly and swoop, soar and sail, on the currents of life, as my father once did. Much remains to be done: "the pendulum swings," and things have been set in motion that urge me forward to put it all out there and give others a connection to illumination and healing. As the daughter of a pilot, I am granted his permission to fly.

GALLERY 1
GROWING UP

First day of kindergarten at Pillsbury School, Minneapolis (age 5 ½)

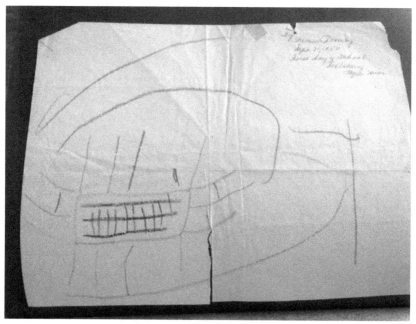

Kindergarten drawing of an A-bomb

Hal and Mary Ravely wedding day, August 30, 1947

Sherrie and Maydris

High school graduation photo and self-portrait, 1941

With my new daddy in Minneapolis

Mother and me, 1947

Nell Flynn Taylor

Sherrie and Nana Lettie Estill in Woolworth's photo booth, 1950s

Banka and Sherrie, 1940s

Christmas 1949 with Lady and Giraffe

Nana Lettie, Margie Ann, Wesley Boyd, and Shannon Estill, 1920s

*Randolph Street house in Enid, Oklahoma, built by my great-grandfather for my
Nana Lettie when she married Banka*

NAME: THE "SHARON ANN"
DATE: MARCH 20,1945
LANDING TIME: 10:45 A.M.
SERIAL NO. ONE
GROSS WEIGHT: 6lbs. 1oz.
WING SPAN: 18 inches
FUEL REQUIREMENTS: LIQUID

THE "ESTILL-BELLE HAS LANDED....
HER MISSION IS COMPLETE....
SHE'LL NEVER BE A FIGHTER
BECAUSE SHE'S FAR TOO SWEET.

PILOT: LT.SHANNON ESTILL

CO-PILOT: MARY TAYLOR ESTILL

Sharon Ann Estill's birth announcement

My very young mother sitting on my parents' first car

Banka, Sherrie, and Nana Lettie in Cedar Rapids, 1940s

DAUGHTERING IN REVERSE

As a daughter born into the arms of anxiety, I stood between my mother's silence and a burning curiosity about my ethereal, ever-perfect father. An enduring conflict existed between underlying feelings of loss—in my extraordinary expectations of those I love, through my fear of abandonment, and in my desire to know why and how things happen. In my struggle to know and recapture lost truth and understanding, I hoped to learn that I was not alone. I wondered about other daughters and sons whose fathers died in war and if they knew, as I did, that we were unique.

Once transcribed, my parents' letters became a portal. In such intimate and careful contact with their words, I knew deep sorrow for the first time. I had no way to avoid what had been awaiting me. These revelations had taken all my life minus three weeks. It was the first whisper of grief that would form the underlayment and bring the tenacity I would need to find my father and bring him home.

The transcribed and sorted letters became a research tool, albeit a sentimental one. I was working on a master's degree in social work with the intention of earning a PhD in psychology, though my agenda was deeper than only esoteric scholarly reasoning. I knew that graduate school required research, and the cardinal rule of choosing a dissertation topic is that it should reflect inquiry about which I felt passionate. It was the only way I could do it at this late date. Though the promise made to my Nana was impetus enough, I needed to resolve my father's uncertain fate.

Embarking on this quest involved a multilayered approach to mystery solving. This mystery involved my father, missing in action and then declared dead at the end of WWII in Europe. Without proof of his demise, my family accepted his fate and moved forward with all questions unanswered. A formal inquiry into the question "What is the effect of father-loss on women whose fathers were killed in war?" (Taylor, 2001) was an effort to seek commonality or disprove it.

Through this research, it was discovered that there is an entire population of war orphans whose American fathers were killed in WWII. Based on that rich and meaningful discovery, I began a search for my father's missing crash site in Germany.

Examining the effect of father-loss in war was a topic I had never unpacked. Knowing there were others of us living with the mystery of our absent fathers, I began reading about father-loss in war. Not surprisingly, little was written, which emboldened me to open the puzzle box and dump out the pieces.

Seeking empirical support for my intuition, I submitted a research proposal to the members of The American War Orphan's Network. I wanted to show how father-loss in war had impacted others in my situation. More than 100 members responded as willing participants. In the end, I narrowed my inquiry to the father-loss experience of daughters. What could be more primal than the original father-daughter connection? Also, I wanted to understand our similarities and differences. Positive response to the study brought with it the realization that I needed to do this work: It was part of my legacy, and I was being urged by seen and unseen forces to ask, "What *is* the lived experience of women whose fathers died in WWII?"

As I selected the women who would accompany me on this inquisitive journey, I chose by instinct and by heart. I will probably never know exactly why the final group of war-orphaned daughters spoke to me or why they were willing to hand me their hearts and their father stories in the process. We are not a group of women who trust easily or who share our fathers willingly without knowing his story is heard with love and respect.

After working as a clinical social worker in Kansas, I found a way to earn a PhD while searching for my father. My first task was to convince a doctoral committee of serious scholars, a colloquium of my peers, and a discerning core advisor that I could accomplish both in less than two years. As a late bloomer approaching 60, I had no time to tarry or get lost in an academic morass. Clearly, the program I chose from the innovative but esteemed Union Institute allowed for scholarship outside traditional rigorous boundaries. I planned to do my fieldwork in Europe, retracing my father's brief career as a fighter pilot. I hoped to find his crash site and make a documentary film about my search for him, though I had no skills or resources for movie making. The search seemed only a matter of paying attention and asking questions of every possible source. I had some skills in doing that, as well as some proven success. Since I was a daughter, I realized that interviewing other daughters would take me back to my experience in which I had a greater field of questions from which to choose.

My doctoral research strengthened and validated my father-quest. It enlightened my sense of purpose which, not that long ago, was a puzzlement. Gradually, it became clear that my purpose has always been to bring forward my father's story, though not as first imagined.

War Orphans

When Ann Bennett Mix, daughter of Pvt. Sydney Bennett (killed in action on April 19, 1945), founded the American WWII Orphans Network (AWON) in 1991, I learned about others whose father-loss mirrored my own. As an AWON member, I learned that I am a WWII war-orphaned daughter. Even though I was fatherless because of the war, I never considered myself an orphan. I had my mother; we took care of each other and held between us the vague presence of my dead father. I always believed that war orphans lived where war happened, not on B Avenue Northeast in Cedar Rapids, Iowa.

Though we were officially designated as war orphans, it seemed ungrateful to think of myself as an orphan when I was told how "lucky" I was to have a new daddy, loving grandparents, a living mother, and, in my case, a brand new name. My new daddy had, after all, married us both! That made him a saint. Still, I wonder: When my father died in the war, why didn't my mother take me on an adventure instead of to Minneapolis with a new daddy?

In the 1980s, I met another daughter whose daddy died in the war, and neither of us knew what to say to the other about the subject. The best we could do was to say, "My daddy died in the war, too." Despite Vietnam and all that ensued between 1945 and then, we knew which war. That assumption would change many wars later. Time and distance from WWII made it necessary to be clear: "My father was killed in WWII."

Indeed, violent death had attached itself to my forever young, smiling father and to my mother's sorrow. I was a child born of a complex soup of family angst and into a world stepping back from the precipice of war.

Ann Bennett Mix and Susan Hadler in *Lost in the Victory* define the status of the children whose fathers were killed in WWII:

> *Since ancient times, fatherless children have been referred to as orphans. In the United States, benefits paid to the fatherless children of war were given to widows and orphans. Yet, cultural ignorance of the existence of war orphans in this country goes so deeply that even those of us who are these orphans are surprised by this designation. After an exhaustive literature search and correspondence with the United States Department of Defense, investigators were stunned to find that no systematic studies on war bereavement were available or had ever been undertaken in the US. (War Federation for Mental Health, 1977)* (xvii)

> *No government agency has a list of the American children whose fathers died in WWII nor do they have statistics on how many there were. This number peaked at over 183,000 and does not include those dependents not receiving benefits because they did not apply for them or because the children were illegitimate. Although benefits have been paid to individual dependents, no records were kept on the orphans themselves. After the children reached eighteen or finished schooling on the G.I. Bill, they disappeared from government records.* (xix)

Among AWON members, I found people who became my friends and siblings, willing to participate in the research that was fueled by my need to know how father-loss in war defines and impacts a daughter's life. I wanted to hear each father-loss experience told in exquisite detail.

It became evident early on that each of us holds a father-story in our hearts that we yearn to tell. These stories, though particular to individual loss, drew the same watery picture from which a small girl emerges. It became evident that war orphans are indeed siblings in the universal family where the father dies in war. The implications were wide and vast. Abraham Lincoln, in his second inaugural address near the end of the Civil War, spoke of the dead soldier's child as his orphan:

With malice toward none: with charity for all: with firmness in the right, as God gives us to see the right, let us strive on to finish the work we are in: to bind up the nation's wounds; to care for him who shall have borne the battle, and for his widow, and his orphan.

Hadler and Mix expounded,

Lincoln's words bring little comfort to WWII orphans, who remain mostly unknown and unnoticed. The government consoled our mothers with monthly checks. Our mothers found us new fathers, who sometimes adopted us, unwittingly denying forever our original identity. Grief and sorrow were expected to be forever hidden in the silence that enfolded us. We withdrew into our fantasies and night terrors not knowing why, but as a way to cope with confusion and mixed messages. Silence characterizes the war orphans' lived experience and intensifies their loss. (xviii)

As an inquisitive child, I was expected to keep my feelings and questions to myself, even though the entire nation was immersed in post-war recovery and jubilation. Reminders were everywhere. I had only to mention my father's name to make his parents cry. If I wanted to see my mother retreat emotionally or look distracted and wistful, I would ask her to tell me about before I was born. If I wanted to impress people with my bravery, I could say, "My daddy died in the war."

I auditioned the powers that my inquiries evoked and remained confused about their impact. I knew then, as I know now, that I missed something fine when I came in as my daddy went out. Early on, I embraced the belief that life would have been better "if only . . ."

Phantom Mothers

Hadler and Mix wrote,

American society influenced by the Victorian values of chastity, self-sacrifice, and family nurturing, defined the lives of the women whom the war widowed. Many women in the 1940s had minimum education, little training, and few job skills. They were unprepared to provide for themselves or for their children. Many moved in with relatives when their men left for war. If the men were killed, many found it necessary to prolong their stay. Some young widows never left their parents' home again. . . .

Among the thousands who died in the last months of the war, many were fathers, leaving their families in grief just as the nation celebrated victory. With or without the "stiff upper lip," some women simply could not deal with life after their husbands were killed. Some became alcoholic, some went insane, and some killed themselves. The children of those mothers often had to parent their mothers and themselves. . . .

At best, it was hard for widows and orphans to "fit in" with the bustling family-oriented post-war society. Married women often perceived young widows without husbands as a threat. Men perceived them as needy. Remarriage helped to take away the war widow stigma. Many widows remarried in haste to give themselves and their children the status and security they needed. Others were able to fall in love again. . . .

Many WWII orphans knew almost nothing about their fathers. Many children were cut off from their paternal family members and from anyone who knew their dads, leaving them dependent on their mothers for knowledge of their fathers. . . .

Many of the mothers lost or destroyed pictures and mementos and memories of their children's fathers. Some upon remarriage changed their children's names. It is as if we are awakened from a dream in which our fathers were lost to us. Perhaps our awakening occurs as we begin to face our own mortality and think about the linkage of our lives, the past and the future. (xx–xxiv)

My mother wrote letters too, though few survived. These, written in the days after he left her to join his army basic training group in Texas, are reminders that they hadn't been apart since they met two years earlier.

2/4/1943

My dear—This scrapbook is for you. I will try and keep a record of all I do and feel while you are away. You've only been gone a few hours, and already I can think of a million ways I could have made you happier. Someday, I want my daughter to read this book. If there is ever another war, I'd like to have her know what waiting for the man she loves really means. Up until your train left tonight, I don't think I had any feeling in me, I was so numb. When you got on the train, I realized you were really leaving me. Believe me, dear, I tried very hard not to show you how I felt. But there at the last, I just couldn't help it. After you left, Frankie didn't think I should go home and sit, so we drove out to the Yacht Club. Oh Honey, it was so lonesome without you.

2/5/1943

This is my first day without you. It seems much longer. I come home from work so exhausted that I go right to bed. When I say good night to you, I concentrate awfully hard and hope that maybe you can hear me.

2/6/1943

This morning I received my first mail from you. I felt one hundred percent better this afternoon. Honey, I only hope you miss me half as much as I miss you. I have talked to your mother every day, but I can't seem to go over and see her; everything over there is so much like you.

These discoveries, filtered through my own experience, were at once disparate and similar. It was as though I were interviewing reunited sisters wrenched from the same enormous family system, framed by early, tragic loss, and anchored (at times insecurely) by intensely grieving and disconnected mothers.

It appears that we are daughters of a distinctive tribe whose men never return from war. In this tribe, some elder women suffer and collapse from the loss; the baby daughters become children before they are infants, teenagers when they are youngsters, and adults instead of adolescents. It is as if we are, as Billy Joel sings, "running on ice."

We are women who feel separate from others, especially in an adopted family setting. We are fearful and anxious and carry a pervasive sense of yearning. Most of us are caretakers and romantics who seek the "ideal" ethereal man who doesn't exist. Embedded in the men we choose is daddy, a daddy substitute, or his antithesis. Our mothers are elusive phantoms, as are our fathers. Our grief remains unresolved and unnamed.

While in Germany, I had a dream about my late sister, Chrissy. She was sitting in my hotel room laughing and said, "Oh ye of little faith. I told you not to worry so much about small stuff." She was right. She wanted to be there, so she got there from heaven, or wherever she traveled a year before.

She remained present as I dug in the dirt on behalf of my father, whom she wished had been her own. We shared our mother but agreed that the woman who raised us became a far different woman after Friday, April 13, 1945. I buried a part of her with my father. The true irony of dreaming about my sister is that she knows everything I can only wonder about. She knows how it is to die, what happens next, and who is really there and in what form. She could tell me what happened after my father's plane crashed; if my parents reunited after our mother died; why she was awarded a difficult father of her own and if they made peace; and most importantly, if she was able to hold her daughter, Mary, once again. She was always the smarter sister.

The War Orphan's Private War

Despite this early-life jolt from childhood reverie into harsh, war-induced reality, we personify depth, wisdom, and resiliency. Each of us carries a private sorrow but has managed to balance it with outward manifestations of creative and empathic expression. There is a sense of relief among us when we are asked to tell our father-stories, followed by healing when attentive and sustained listening validates the story. It is surprising that each story is traditionally laced with fear and caution, as well as a distinct sense of pride and joy—all testifying to the power of disclosure.

It's true that many of us never learned to be daughters in the pure sense of having a father to guide us. Some of us never realized the nurturing touch of a father or how to recognize the buffer zone between danger and ourselves. Somehow, in the twisted remnants of life in the post-war 1950s, we, along with our mothers, were disregarded and expected to cope as adults in a shattering shift of reality. We did, but not without a fight. Some only realized in midlife that their fathers were not the only family hero(ine). We, too, survived a war of unending emotional proportion, as did our mothers.

To lose a father in war becomes a flat fact of life until women like those who entrusted me with their precious secrets, fantasies, longings, and hopes step forward. In coming forth, they risk what I sought to learn. They are each whole unto themselves despite their initially abrupt disconnection from what they believe would have been a perfect love. Each speaks of a trauma that takes its toll and offers little recompense for what was lost.

The themes that continued to emerge from my research stand deep and dark, flowing with a perpetual insistence throughout our lives. They are either surprising in clarity or subtle in the way they blend with the nuances of life. The birthing of these themes would not be a simple matter, but one of teasing and coaxing them from the darkest places, some unknown, all unlit. They are what lie beneath—what illuminates what was lost in WWII.

FROM TRANSCRIPTION
TO DISCOVERY

O n one occasion, my father wrote of a dream he had that would one day be captured on canvas by the artist James Hartel:

2/14/1945

Sweetheart: In this dream, which I promised to describe in my V-mail note, you and I, it seems, were bob-o-links, and our baby was, quite naturally, a baby bob-o-link.

All day long, we'd rat race over San Francisco Bay, just the three of us, and have a wonderful time, until the raven entered the scene. A huge black bird, she was instantly attracted by our baby and even went so far as to say the little devil looked good enough to eat. Well, not long later, she determined to do just that, because she took out after the poor little thing.

Because of the difference in size and weight, the baby could outrun the attacker; but because of our small size, we were unable to drive off the intruder. Finally, in desperation, I remembered our friend, the bald eagle, who lived in the hills. I rushed up to secure his services. He gladly accompanied me. And as we flew bayward, I took pains to explain the situation. However, drawing near the bay, we heard the wee one singing merrily away, so the eagle decided we'd not need him and started back for his home.

Then, I perceived what had occurred. The raven had caught the babe but, seeing the eagle approach, decided the most subtle course of action would be to threaten the sprout until it burst into frenzied song. I discovered the truth of the matter in time to call the eagle back and save our little one by the simple expedient of knocking the intruder from the sky, freeing our baby.

This should be definite proof that I'm kind of nutz. Guess putting it all in writing is dangerous, because this sort of thing is almost grounds for divorce. Anyway, I have a big time when I dream. They are like a three-ring circus and a new show each time. Hmmmmmm.

The transcription of my parents' letters set me upon a path that would reveal the picture on the puzzle box, solving the puzzlement. Their lives, together and apart, were full of people, events, preferences, book and film reviews, flirting, yearning, and history. Somehow, my father managed to receive Book of the Month Club selections sent to a Belgian chateau even during a war. My mother had a companion subscription. Their separate but matching subscriptions to *Time* and *Reader's Digest* led to spirited written discussions of current events. My mother kept her subscriptions for the rest of her life. I remember canceling them with great sorrow after she died.

Their reading preferences were identical in history, biography, poetry, and memoir. It was easy for me to read the books they read and discussed in their letters because some of them were in my library. Each book contains my father's personalized bookplate on the frontispiece—a sailing ship in a stormy sea, depicted in shades of sepia. He describes it in a letter to my mother:

Oh yes! I ordered some bookplates—you know, gummed paper with an etching or some appropriate sort of illustration printed with Ex Libris—from the library of—and, of course, my name. [It] is a fine etching of a full-rigged sailing vessel.

My parents called each other Scootie and Gener, among other nicknames typical of the era and wartime correspondence. My mother wrote to him about movies she saw and music she listened to on the radio. They discussed music that reminded them of each other—Glen Miller's "In the Mood" was their favorite song, but they loved to listen and dance to Tommy Dorsey and Guy Lombardo. She, like many women on the homefront, was a Frank Sinatra fan. My father's opinion of Frank Sinatra was dubious, as he described him as "a wolf who can't sing or go to war." While Sinatra was beloved by men and women alike, those who had enlisted didn't appreciate his lack of war service.

8/14/1943

Just read an article in this week's Time on your lover, Frank Sinatra. He apparently sang in the Hollywood Bowl, and to quote Time, "as an Army sergeant cracked, 'hope they don't forget to flush the bowl.'"

Their earliest letters, written when he traveled for John Deere Farm Implement Company after graduation, were a carefree flurry of weekend plans and loan arrangements with his parents as he bought his first car for less than $100. It was a fine, green Plymouth into which they would put five cents worth of gas and head to the Yacht Club to dance and have romantic dinners. He planned to go to college, and he loved to buy her gifts, including a new riding crop and "denim pants." One of his last letters bears testimony to what life was denying them:

12/24/44, Christmas Eve in Belgium

My own very dearest: Don't really have anything of importance to say tonight, but I just had to talk to you for a few minutes, darlin'. I suppose if I were home we would be helping Pop with his Christmas shopping and simply taking one another for granted. Some folks just can't see the forest for the trees, I guess. Then, we would probably go to your Mom's for a while, and perhaps to the Yacht Club—all this time, mind you, being very casual and calm about everything. That is, if I weren't here. Well, by heaven, next Christmas, I'll be with you, darlin', if I must drag you half way around the world to accomplish my end. I just pray that this whole damn mess will be over by the next birthday of Our Lord and, God willing, we are together again. And together for good. Words fail to express how we feel about these crew chiefs and their boys. Why tonite, on Christmas Eve, they're out on the line working on the ships with flashlights for their only companions. If we pilots can just be worthy of our crew chiefs, everything will be OK. They take better care of those ships than if they were flying them personally.

As she converted to Catholicism, he wrote out the prayers she would need to know, and he told her about a rosary and a St. Christopher medal for flyers that he was mailing home:

1/26/1945

Went to the Abbey for Mass Sunday last and afterwards got to shop around for a rosary for you. Didn't see anything I especially liked until Fr. Francis produced the ones with gold and silver links! (The kind that would cost $10-$15 in those wonderful States.) I spotted the one I liked for you, then upon further study of the situation, one for Mom and one for Midget [his sister, Margie]. Also, found you a tiny reproduction of the St. Christopher flyer's medal I wear.

He spent time—when not flying or letter writing—at the abbey gift shop or visiting with the abbey nuns. As he writes about the protective properties of saints, his devotion to his church is apparent. He added the small icons of saintly protection in his plane, including the flier's medal he always wore. Unfortunately, he wasn't flying his plane on the day he was shot down. The irony is not lost on his daughter. Another "what if?" line is added to the mental list.

2/23/1945

Bought a special St. Christopher medal at the Abbey yesterday and had Sgt. Ham secure it to the control column on my big iron bird as an anti-flak device. I'll wager that when good St. Christopher went about aiding the travelers of his day, he didn't ever dream, in his wildest imaginings, that he'd have to help some bird driver kick his airplane around. He's on the surface controls; St. Theresa helps on the throttles and keeps the bloomin' engines running. I just sit there dumb and happy, thinking of immortal remarks to make over the air . . .

He accounted for his pilot and hazardous duty pay in money orders sent home and urged my mother to buy anything she needed. They were preparing financially for the life they would enjoy when he returned. He wrote often of the airline he wanted to start with his brother-in-law, my Uncle Clark Chandler. At the least, he promised, he would buy a plane in which he would fly us all over the country on grand adventures.

I listed my favorite letters by dates and main topics and cross-referenced his illustrations and drawings the same way. For example, "Three world leaders, pencil and ink wash drawing, 1942, Hotel Russell-Lamson, Waterloo, Iowa, stationery."

Their intimacy was contained in their letters. Separated by preparing for war and going to war, my parents probably spent less than a month sleeping in the same bed. But for the letters, their story, though brief, would leave precious little evidence of its existence. I made lists of the books they read, the music they liked, and the people they knew. A name that my father mentioned throughout his time in Belgium and finally Germany was Henry Ham, his crew chief. Henry Ham, a fellow Iowan, was surprisingly easy to find after 50 years. When he called in response to my letter, his memories of my father were distinct and evocative:

> I waited all night for your dad's plane to come back. I wouldn't leave because I believed his plane would appear in the sky at any minute. He was the only guy in the squadron with a baby. I never got over that empty runway. His own plane was there, you know, because we'd pulled it off the line the day before . . . he was flying a borrowed bird. Finally, they made me leave when they all came to fly the next morning. Your father was the best man and pilot I ever knew. He would have been the best father too.

After I spoke with Ham, I found a letter from my father describing a project he was working on with Ham. He wanted his plane nose art replaced and told my mother how he envisioned it:

4/3/1945

Am having "Honeybunch" painted on my ship tomorrow. Ham is going to paint an ear of Iowa corn on the other side of the gondola, and his assistant, Sgt. Nelson, is going to add a Texas jackrabbit gnawing on the corn.

He was killed 10 days later, and the nose art was never completed. More than a half century later, Dutch artist Henrik Jacobsson visited my website and said he'd like to make a model of my father's plane with the nose art as my father wished. He created a beautiful miniature P-38, correct in every detail, including my father's name on the side of the plane. I love that little pilot designation—so modern yet timeless. He would have been proud to be identified as the pilot of his P-38 in just that way.

Henry Ham told a heartbreaking story interspersed with sweet remembrances about my father's generosity with his crew and how he would work with them on the flight line to get his "ship" in perfect flying condition. A bottle of French brandy or local wine would show up in the crew quarters, and they always knew it was from my father. To say a pilot and his crew chief depended on each other would underestimate the skill and dedication that defines their relationship. Henry Ham waited for my father to return from his last flight long after the rest of his squadron returned with the report that Lt. Estill's plane had sustained a direct hit and exploded.

Since my father owned two leather A-2 flying jackets, he gave one to Sgt. Ham. He told him to wear it after the war to remind him that he was an equally important part of the ultimate victory. After the war, Ham got as far as the US military checkpoint with my father's precious A-2 jacket, which he intended to give to my mother, when it was taken away from him because it belonged to an officer. My mother never knew how close she came to holding her husband's favorite possession. There are many things I've discovered that would have increased my mother's despair. My father wrote about his A-2 jacket in a line of one of his letters:

> *We get to keep our A-2 jackets upon our return to the States. I'm thankful for that because I'd rather part with almost any other item of equipment.*

Despite these incremental losses commingled with the sparkling evidence of my father's brief existence, his crew chief's next disclosure balanced the scales of injustice. He told me that my father's squadron was still meeting for regular reunions. He must have made a few calls, because the next day, I had the first of countless conversations with my father's squadron mates. They became my "adopted dads" of the 474th Fighter Group.

I miss that lost A-2 jacket, but in knowing these men, I've gained more than a precious leather jacket by which to know and touch my father's memory. Still, I would have loved that old jacket with my father's name hand-painted (by him) on the front over his heart. I have pictures of him wearing it, and if I examine it carefully, I can almost feel him under the buttery brown leather.

When my son, Justin Rocca, was in high school, I gave him a replica of his grandfather's A-2 jacket ordered from an Air Force catalogue. He wore it every day until his broad shoulders outgrew it. He always carried two of his grandfather's squadron patches in the secret inside pocket, even to hockey practice.

As my father's crew chief emerged fully formed from the letters, I received a phone call from Jack Zaverl. Jack had been one of my father's closest squadron friends, and he was the first to contact me as soon as he heard I was searching for my father. I sent him his first Father's Day card. He was overwhelmed and always called me "Daughter!"

Thus, I became the long-lost and now-found daughter of the remaining 474th fighter pilots. In knowing them, I would know my father in a way that expresses my love for him and for them. It was Henry Ham who opened the door to these relationships that would last for decades and throughout the many "last flights" these dear men would take after they shared their stories, lives, and wisdom with this grateful daughter.

This precious association with my father's squadron (428th) and with the members of the other two squadrons (429th and 430th) that comprised the 474th Fighter Group brought me comfort and joyous connection to my father. Some of them watched him fall to the earth, and they still cry as they remember. Through each precious piece of information wrapped in a distant memory, I gained the courage to search for my father's crash site and to bring him home. I did it for my father, for my mother, for his parents, for his squadron mates, and, of course, for "Mike."

My father offered his opinion of the fighter group logo:

12/30/1944

Am enclosing the remainder of the squadron insignia cards promised you. I still can't imagine why the artist pictured a wolf-like creature at the controls. A timid little lamb would really be much more appropriate.

When I found the 474th Fighter Group, one of my father's squadron friends and a fellow Iowan, Bill Capron, started making plans. He lived in Phoenix with his Cedar Rapids high school sweetheart and new wife, Lois. Lois and my mother graduated a year apart from Franklin High, and she reflected my mother in time and history. Once I showed her a picture of my mother, and she said she had the same dress, which she bought at Craemer's Department Store where my Nana Nell worked.

Bill and my father flew many missions together—including the last—and he'd never forgotten the terrible day my father was shot down. He said he knew him well, loved him as a friend, and wanted to be the first of my adopted dads of the 474th to welcome Shannon's daughter into the group. Bill was shot down over France, where a French farmer hid him in order to escape Nazi capture. They gave him a beret, which he wore often to remind him of his good fortune. It was a story he loved to tell, and I loved to hear. He stepped into my life as one of the surrogate fathers who scooped me up into a world I had been missing all my life. It was a world of people who knew, loved, and flew with my father. With each frontline story, with each remembrance of a small thing that connected the dots for me about my father, every tiny detail was accompanied by a puzzle piece that I carefully placed with the others. There is a debt of gratitude attached to the smallest and most grand gestures and conversations I've had with this group. Of the original 150 I found in 1993, only a few remain, but I hold dear the friendships with those who knew my father and whom I considered my adopted dads.

The Champlin Air Museum at Falcon Field in Mesa, Arizona, was not yet open for the day, but Bill had arranged for us to have early admission. We were led into the massive hangar still resonating with the silenced engines of a pristine collection of WWII warplanes. We walked beneath their massive wings toward a distinctive silver plane with twin engines and a boom on the tail, alike in appearance and function to a racing car's rear spoiler. We stood in the shadow of a restored P-38 Lightning.

They boosted me up the slim ladder at the back of the plane and into the cockpit, where Bill buckled me into the pilot's seat and closed the Plexiglas canopy. As my father before me, I sat for a whisper of time in the plane he loved to fly. The window high above the canopy framed the high, blue desert sky, connecting plane to flight, a daughter to her father.

At that moment, I asked my father to help me find him and sort out the puzzle of his absence. Each precious piece of information, wrapped in a distant memory and shared by my father's squadron, gave me the courage to search for my father's crash site and believe that I would bring him home. This one was the first but not the last. For this precious welcome and our subsequent friendship, I will always love Bill Capron and remember this auspicious day of our first meeting in a quiet airplane hangar.

I had no idea how I would get from sitting in a P-38 cockpit in Arizona to discovering my father's crash site from 1945. My father's squadron friends were willing partners in my father-quest, and this was a good start.

GALLERY 2
WWII

Precious war correspondence

Jack Downer, Mary Taylor Estill, Shannon Estill

Wedding day 1943, Ft. Stockton, TX

A personalized bookplate from my father's library

Kissing a John Deere tractor in honor of his pre-war job

Château le Beauchêne, front and chapel side view

MIA and KIA telegrams

My father and his A-2 jacket

Artist James Hartel's illustration of the Golden Gate Bridge dream

Three world leaders, 1942

Crew Chief Henry Ham (left) with unknown P-38 mechanic

1st Lt. Bill Capron, 1944   *Bill Capron in the Champlin Air Museum*

Favorite photo of young pilot, 1st Lt. Jack Zaverl

IRELAND TO BELGIUM
TO GERMANY

What ties it together is the suggestion of loss, of disappearance, and of longing. (The Gravity of Birds, Tracy Guzeman)

I n a circuitous quirk of fate, one of my squadron "dads," Lloyd Wenzel, connected me with a Belgian researcher who recommended that I find a researcher in Germany, because he was limited to searching for planes shot down in Belgium. We knew my father's plane had gone down in East Germany. Dick Uhley, a P-38 pilot and "droop snoop photographer" who rode in a special pod below the P-38 on photo reconnaissance missions, knew a German researcher who locates WWII planes shot down in Germany. It was amazing enough that someone with that specific interest even existed. I was assured that Hans-Guenther Ploes was the best person for the job of finding a very small needle in a large German haystack.

I could only attribute this confluence of fortuitous events to mysterious and mischievous forces. As I embarked on the road to locating an obscure and mostly forgotten crash site, I was not alone.

I was three weeks into my travels around Ireland, Belgium, Holland, and Germany, where I was geographically retracing the last months of my father's life. I started in Ireland because that's our shared heritage and also to attend a professional conference aptly titled "Jung in Ireland: A Rich Tapestry, Midlife and Beyond." I was certain my father would approve of this diversion from his itinerary, as it seemed an appropriate way to celebrate my birthday.

One free day from the conference, I boarded a bus with racing Irish setters on either side to the nearby peninsula town of Dingle. I found another Irish setter bus that traveled through glorious countryside and villages. By the time I returned to the hotel that night, I hadn't spoken a word all day. When I did, it was to order a celebratory whiskey at the bar; it was my 56th birthday.

I wanted to stand in the places where my father lived and flew in Belgium and Germany; to the American Cemetery in Margraten, Holland, where his name is inscribed on the Tablets of the Missing; and to the airfield from whence he flew his last mission. My hope was to find Château le Beauchêne (where my father lived with his squadron), the Benedictine Abbey of Maredret (where he went to Mass and befriended the nuns), and the former Louie's Pub and Barber Shop in Falaën, Belgium (where the squadron spent time between flying missions). My father's letters were full of illuminating descriptions of these sites.

My first opportunity to find the chateau was while on a trip to Europe in 1972. I showed photos of the chateau from my parents' photo album to anyone in Brussels who might know a little history and a few who didn't. I was sent to visit Countess Marie Caroline d'Ursel, who had written a small book about Belgian chateaus. We spent a day visiting possible chateau sites. Sadly, we never even came close. How I would have loved to see where my father lived with his friend Don Collins in the uppermost part of the chateau. I wanted to stand at the grand entrance and see what he saw when he arrived there in 1944. Mostly, I wanted to sit where he had written letters to my mother and to stand in the stillness of time and imagine that the spirit of the 428th Fighter Squadron lingered there.

Thirty years after the first failed attempt to find the chateau, I was carrying a collection of maps drawn in exquisite detail by Jack Zaverl, who remembered what was where in 1945. As an engineer, he knew something about logistics. As an historic mapmaker, he was accurate and exact. Sadly, the chateau had been demolished in the 1970s, close to the first time I was trying and failing to find it.

As I embarked upon this journey that closely followed my father's last days, the revelations would be life defining for me. How could I know that I would get close enough to touch my father, if not in body, then in spirit and energy? I hoped that much would be revealed, along with the history of WWII Germany. I carried hope with me as I navigated the past while hoping to make sense of the present.

THE QUEST BEGINS

As I set out on March 1, 2001, I had an overwhelming sense of meeting my father's spirit and bringing him back with me at the end. Were my mother buried somewhere, I would have taken him to her. I could only believe I was always meant to do this, called to do it, destined at this time in my life. This purposeful trip was a portal into an alternate reality.

Mom would love this, I thought. It still amazes me that she never did things like I do for myself. Certainly she wasn't a woman less rebellious than I. By the time I was hers, she was mine. Her heart and soul had been buried beneath the deepest war rubble. Whether she tried to get out, or if she did save herself in the only way she knew, I'll never know. While I'll never know my father, I feel as though I know her less intimately. But, I believe that her spirit was left beneath the tossed landscape of her life, and she only retrieved part of it.

1/15/1945

We also had a lengthy argument on the morals of womanhood. These are my contentions: Any girl is essentially good, pure of mind and heart, so to speak, and becomes only bad through environment or other influences. Also, I insist that very few, if any, girls realize that almost every man's thoughts go somewhat like this: "I can sleep with this woman, and if she refuses to acquiesce, she is surely mad." The opposition disagreed in this regard: "Some are bad, some are good due to personality traits, and most girls do realize such sinister thoughts, as outlined above, do exist. Their strongest argument was the foolhardy faith that the average girl places in a man when she drinks promiscuously in the company of a man, particularly when circumstances are propitious to seduction. Guess, perhaps, I'm slightly daft but am still old fashioned enough to adhere to my beliefs.

Upon arrival in Brussels, I called Hans-Guenther, who was waiting in Aachen, to give him my arrival schedule in Germany. I tried each payphone along the wall of the Gare du Midi train station in Brussels but failed miserably. I had about given up when I noticed a Belgian phone card still in a card slot of the last phone. It had just enough euros left to make one call, which I later deemed the first of the amazements I would experience on this quest, along with finding a reproduction of a 1945 calendar at the newsstand.

I stepped off the Thalys train from Brussels in Aachen, Germany, to enter the unusual but fortuitous world of Hans-Guenther Ploes, the famous German air historian. We recognized each other from our descriptions and a few photos. I remember thinking that he was younger than I expected, and it was possible he would change my world. His English was perfect, and he seemed happy to meet me and find a place for dinner so we could plan our travels. He had ideas about where we should go and in what order, and I agreed—with no idea of the outcome. I never questioned my good fortune to have his attention to the many details that would have to coalesce in order to find a long-lost crash site. I not only found him easy to be with but also incredibly knowledgeable. We laughed together; he was brilliant about many things.

Thus, my destiny shifted once again, and I hoped he would help me write the story of my father's last flight. To call him knowledgeable in matters of WWII aircraft would be minimizing his level of knowing and discounting his ability to see what lies beneath the surface of a field, a bog, or a forest in a snowstorm. He wanted me to see Germany as more than the former political enemy of the United States. Hans-Guenther and the people we met over the next weeks became my teachers, and Germany my field research lab. Searching for my father's crash site was but the essential center of what had become our quest. There were many roads to travel before we would end up where it began in 1945.

Field Notes, 3/25/2001—*My impressions are, in a word, German. I doubt that I'll ever live easily on the soil where my father died. Or forget about the unseen hands that killed rather than be killed. Is there a difference, I wonder, between that kind of murder and any other? This murder was justified by war, which necessitates killing.*

The next day, Hans-Guenther and I visited the Margraten American Cemetery in Holland, where my father's name is engraved on the Tablets of the Missing. Until I met the men of my father's squadron, I had no idea that he was remembered with a flower wreath every Memorial Day.

It was cold that day as Hans-Guenther walked with me to the wall. I was determined to touch my father's name and witness this proof for myself. Apparently, members of my father's brother's family had visited Margraten, but no one told me about this monument. We found paper and pencils in the cemetery office and did a rubbing of my father's name, which I rolled up and carried with me for the duration of my trip.

I asked the cemetery director why some of the names had brass rosettes next to them. He told me they were those who were found and no longer missing in action. I told Hans-Guenther we would return with a rosette for my father's name as someone took hopeful pictures of us standing by the wall. We returned to the rental car and headed back to Germany to accomplish the improbable.

"Mom, you know what you know, when you know what you know," my young son Justin once said. I remembered his cryptic message when I realized I would soon learn about the country where my father died and how it fit into my life's puzzle. I was about to find out what I knew that I needed to know.

In our travels through Germany, Hans-Guenther and I divided our time, whether by accident or design, in this manner: 30 percent driving on the Autobahn at speeds I learned not to convert from kilometers to miles per hour, and 5 percent eating at McDonald's, searching for water without bubbles for me and for Haribo Goldbären Gummi Bears. We consulted maps 10 percent of the time, which Hans-Guenther laboriously marked to include each detour and side trip. In the end, we traversed five huge, specially selected, and exquisitely detailed maps with which a small room could be wallpapered. He marked our route along the way so I wouldn't forget where we'd been and what remained to be explored. For another 20 percent, we met with people who in some obscure or obvious way knew about WWII aircraft or who belonged to a group of researchers. Each had a sliding scale of valuable information about which Hans-Guenther had endless questions.

We trekked through ancient forests, bogs, and fields of East and West Germany 25 percent of the time with a metal detector and a roll of plastic collecting bags, which were carefully marked and filled with aircraft pieces. Buried aircraft and pilots were identified, sometimes for the first time. A final 10 percent was allotted for spontaneous sightseeing that included complex and fascinating German history lessons. Each day of travel and exploration ended with good German wine, more conversation, and, on the last day, a double rainbow.

As we began our trip to Weimar, we drove through a construction site at the Aachener Highway junction. Somehow, a caution sign cleanly removed the rental car's outside mirror. An auspicious beginning to our day. We earned a slight delay for repairs.

JOURNEY TO WEIMAR, THE CULTURAL CITY OF EUROPE

The Global City Map website describes Weimar as a city with vast cultural heritage:

It is most often recognized as the place where Germany's first democratic constitution was signed after the First World War, giving its name to the Weimar Republic period in German politics, of 1918 to 1933. However, the city was also the focal point of the German Enlightenment and home of the leading characters of the literary genre of Weimar Classicism, the writers Goethe and Schiller. The city was also the birthplace of the Bauhaus movement, founded in 1919 by Walter Gropius, with artists Wassily Kandinsky, Paul Klee, Oskar Schlemmer, and Lyonel Feininger teaching in Weimar's Bauhaus School. Many places in the city center have been designated as UNESCO World Heritage sites.

Hans-Guenther described it similarly as we walked the streets of Weimar, where evidence of the bombed and restored town center is memorialized in books and pamphlets with shocking before-and-after-the-bombing photos. The Rund um den Marktplatz was destroyed by Allied bombs but for the apothecary. Though the square is rebuilt, the shadow of its former self remains a memory overlay of the truth of war. Weimar is a center of culture in arts and music that became a particularly onerous target.

The next day, we spent a dark and uncomprehending morning at what remains of Buchenwald Concentration Camp,near Weimar. Few original buildings remain except for the camp gate with its infamous inscription: Jedem das Seine (To Each His Own). From a Weimar tourist pamphlet,

> *Weimar stands for the opposites of humanism and barbarianism. The German definition of culture and its ideals are just as closely entwined with this city, as are the terrors of National Socialism. Weimar's glory ends at Ettersberg hill, where the concentration camp Buchenwald was built in 1937. Over 56,000 people died there—were shot, starved, or died of illness—only a few kilometers from Ettersburg Castle, Anna Amalia's "court of muses." Today, the Buchenwald Memorial at the former concentration camp maintains the memory of the horror on Ettersberg Hill. The prisoners' camp later operated by the Soviets also belongs to the history presented here.*

Prisoners built a zoo constructed as a leisure garden for the families of the SS guards. The bear enclosure remains evil evidence of the inequity and injustices of war. We drove away knowing we could.

This somber history is connected to my quest to find my father's crash site through the necessity to understand Germany when we were the enemy. It helped me sort out some of the vagaries and consequences of war. I knew why my father and others like him were willing to die to protect us from a similar fate. Clearly, Germany had been devastated.

Field Notes, 3/28/2001—*I am drowning in yummy quilts and pillows on a high bed of feathers and soft cotton sheets. The Elephant is a hotel built in the 1600s that somehow survived the war and the bombs that destroyed most of the town square. This is the former East Germany, and evidence of war lingers as though preserved forever under glass. It is how I am deeply aware of WWII history. My doctoral dissertation will be the final portrait of these days. All the quirky parts and side trips, people and places, but this is the most magic place of all. Elephants go way back to my baby history when Banka drew me elephants with the mechanical pencil he kept in his shirt pocket. Those elephants created a lifelong talisman for me, and now, in this place so far from my world but so close to my father's, there are elephants everywhere. Banka wrote me stories about my world, typed on his Underwood typewriter. Only two have been preserved, and one is about my daddy from his daddy's perspective.*

As my German WWII education continued, it was clear that we were touching all sides of the war. I idly wondered if the gunner who shot down my father's plane had a daughter. My primary challenge, however, was to listen to lengthy German conversations. As an only child for seven years, I had honed my skills as an observer of adult behavior and conversation, also lost in translation. As a therapist, I learned to interpret nuance and to manage silence. Despite my patient exterior, I remained ever vigilant for the German word "vater," which I knew to mean father. I believed that this strange route, in conjunction with Hans-Guenther's skills and intuition, would lead me to my father. It was well worth 20 percent of my time to simply absorb the possibility of what we would discover and to be more like an owl and less like my usual hummingbird self.

After ruling out Roitzsch Bog as a possible crash site, we moved on to a distant, silent, and muddy forest. Hans-Guenther found a crashed ME109 but no evidence of a pilot.

The next day, March 31, 2001, though not a part of the search, brought me closer to my father as I stood where my father stood during his last moments on earth. The Ollheim/ Strassfield airstrip, just outside of Euskirchen, is a forest of then-56-year-old trees. The concrete of the runway was blown up after my father's group left in 1945. Bomb craters litter the landscape. Pieces of runway concrete lie everywhere, frosted with mosses and lichen.

Hans-Guenther introduced me to Herr Franz-Josef Kessler, then in his late 70s, who was in charge of the airfield when the ground echelon of the 474th FG took over. My father's fighter group moved in on April 10, 1945. Herr Kessler remembered that the squadron tents were near the airstrip and were mired in spring mud.

The runway had become a forest, but I could easily picture it when my father's plane flew east for his last flight. I was sad that he spent the last three days of his life sleeping on muddy ground where I stood that afternoon, as the sun was setting at the far end of the invisible airstrip. I sensed the presence of the Germans who fought for and lost so much, including this piece of land in the former West Germany.

A TEMPORARY
FAREWELL

Hans-Guenther's apartment in Aachen is a rare-objects museum full of salvaged airplane parts. He could identify the plane type, crash site, and whether the pilot survived or not because he had laboriously cataloged each part and piece. He would show me a diagram in the particular airplane parts catalogue that determined where the part fit on a plane.

But it was the personal stuff that I noticed: a glove thumb, goggle lenses, buttons, buckles and straps, parachute silk. Each is labeled with a tiny white encoded sticker. Mostly, he carries it all in his head.

My father's plane and crash date were added to Hans-Guenther's lists, but many squares on the grid were still empty. Hans-Guenther wondered if my father's plane, which he wasn't flying the day he was killed, might have ended up in the Ollhiem/Strassfield bunkers where American pilots were ordered to destroy and bury P-38s after the war. Herr Kessler's interest was in excavating the bunkers and assembling a P-38 cockpit. It seemed that everything we were seeking or finding were pieces of a whole, just like the puzzle.

We walked along what is left of the Western Wall in Aachen: a complex arrangement of stones and leftover razor wire. Hans-Guenther told me it was booby trapped with land mines in an intricate and impenetrable grid of concrete pillars. The Germans were, and still are, resourceful and determined.

As our time together ended, we were only marginally closer to finding my father's crash site. I remained hopeful and more informed about the odds of discovery. Also, I knew a significant amount of history along with the friendship of an expert who understood the power of my need to know. It was mutual and enlightening for us, but mostly for me.

I returned to working on my PhD with determination to further explore whatever emerged from Germany. Doctoral work included a run-up to writing my dissertation, preceded by attending required seminars, workshops, meetings, navigating the committee approval process, teaching in the social work department at Arizona State University, supervising and advising interns, and working with my committee faculty chair on my evolving dissertation.

Field Notes, 4/13/2001

Dearest Gener:

This has truly been your year. I am so close to finding you; I feel it on the deepest level. Your plane and mortal evidence have been in Germany all my life. With your continued guidance, I'll be able to see what only you have known about what happened 56 years ago today. I sensed you at every turn on my trip to Europe—even in Ireland—even now. This seems to be my legacy, doesn't it? Well, you bequeathed it to me, and I know it's possible to bring you home. It's symbolic, of course, bringing you home, but apt symbolism indeed. Things determined impossible are made possible. That is my mission. I am supported by so many who care about you, about me, about our story. I've stayed busy with you, my phantom father, for a very long time; though it feels like you really revealed yourself when I became immersed in transcribing your letters. I learned that I needed to be relentless in making this path through an overgrown airstrip. You stood there for the last time the day you never returned. I stood there too and realized the sacredness of the space. With your expert flying and my navigating, we should touch down on the runway of our creation. With your insistent touch on the rudder of my life, I'll finish my doctoral work; and when I graduate, that will be for us. All the earthly living and learning is because of you and Mom. I thank you both for that spirit and strength.

This past year has been poignant in many ways. I'm not telling you anything you don't know, but it helps seeing what I think. So much of my little mother comes through in ways I know and love. I hope you two are finally together or at least understand why our time was so brief.

One of your last letters to Mom was dated Easter 1945. Tomorrow is Easter, 56 years later, and we will have dinner with Bill Capron and his wife, Lois. Do you remember him? He remembers you and has taken very good care of me, as have many of your old squadron friends. Lloyd Wenzel, Howard Darnell, Paul Meier, Jack Zaverl, Paul Hissey, and, of course, Cy Cardiff, who still plays hockey. Thank you, by the way, for the glorious connection to HG. He's some kind of angel. He communicates via his instincts and lots of experience with crash-site recovery. Who does that? Apparently, he has appeared in my life just for this purpose. Also, he's a good friend, and I love spending time with him. You choose all the men in my life so well.

Justin starts high school this year, and I'd like to requisition some high-level protection while he's getting world smart. He's an *interesting, complex soul. Help him stay out of the turbulence, as possible.*

On this auspicious anniversary of your departure, your job remains as my copilot, occasionally as my wingman, but forever as my father. I need you, I love you, and I'm a pursuit pilot hot on your trail. Keep us safe, and watch the sky when I forget I am flying and we drop a few thousand feet. I'll make you proud of me and proud of my tenacity and spirit. I got it from you and Mom, so take credit. I miss you every day but especially this one.

With love from your daughter, Sharon Estill Taylor

DISCOVERY AND RECOVERY: THE IMPOSSIBLE MADE POSSIBLE

Does the earth remember? Do these fields, upon which unspeakable carnage occurred, where unkowable numbers of bodies are buried, bear witness in some way? And if they do, with what voice do they speak? Is there a numinous presence of death in these now placid battlefields, these places of stilled time? (Hold Still: A Memoir with Photographs, Sally Mann)

Two years later, Hans-Guenther invited me to return to Germany. I flew into Leipzig where we met at the airport. He seemed uncharacteristically mysterious. When I asked him what was up, he instructed me to be patient. "Tonight at dinner, I have something to show you. Now, we have a new crash site to check out."

Also, our team of two had grown by two in my absence. One of them, a retired German engineer, Ernst Eberle, spoke perfect English with a lovely British accent and knew more about my father than I expected. He became not only a dear friend but also my most attentive and willing translator. I was again listening to intense German conversations punctuated with the cadence of eyewitness accounts of war plane crashes. Due to Ernst's patient translation, I knew what was being said. The only other woman, a welcome addition, was Waltraud (Wally) Busch, notetaker and rock collector.

Along with this group of like-minded, historically inquisitive Germans, plus the usual locals, I spent the afternoon in a forest with metal detectors, plastic collection bags, and walking, stopping, and talking. Any clear recollection of our success at that wooded site was eclipsed by what I would learn that evening. Since there seemed to be an atypical sense of anticipation among the team members, I asked Ernst if the crash site we were working on was my father's.

His response was to implore my patience. I could only conclude that I was hovering around a discovery of another kind. To do my time at this site was a goodwill offering for what was to come. Things began to feel surreal, but nothing could prepare me for what would be revealed as a result of Hans-Guenther's astonishing resourcefulness over the past two years, along with his extensive understanding of history.

At the end of the day, we left the site and headed back to Torgau. We decided to meet in my suite on the top floor of the century-old Central Hotel.

Hans-Guenther arrived that evening with Ernst and Wally. He had his P-38 aircraft parts catalogue, which I'd seen while visiting his Aachen apartment. He also carried a package wrapped in dirty plastic. He opened the catalogue to a spreadsheet of numbers that identified a lead weight for an aileron stabilizer from a P-38J, the plane my father flew on the day he was shot down. He carefully unwrapped the plastic package as dirt drifted onto the parts catalogue.

"See this?" he said, placing it into my hands. "There are numbers stamped on the side of the part which tell us that this part number matches this catalogue description. This part is the aileron counterbalance weight from your father's plane." He pointed to the faint identifying stamp on the piece in my hands and then to matching numbers on the parts catalogue page.

Shadowed by even greater emotion, we cried together. Then we had wine. Even though part of my brain realized what I was seeing, I had been transported to a place where I struggled to connect the data with an appropriate response, an unusual occurrence for me.

As I was flying to Leipzig that morning, Hans-Guenther had, by process of elimination and eyewitness interviews, discovered what he believed to be the field where my father's plane crashed. On the surface where they had only to collect it, clean it off, and read the matching numbers, they found the piece I was holding. It was hard for me to give it back so it could be preserved with the pieces retrieved that morning. I negotiated its custody for that night, and I slept with it on the next pillow. Later, as I tried, but mostly failed, to fall asleep, I realized that this lumpy, gray part was encouragement from my parents from wherever they watched and guided their daughter through this quest. Symbolically, the aileron stabilizer is essential to the wings as my father is essential to me.

Before I slept, I wrote to my father in my journal:

Field Notes, 3/15/2003—*Tonight, I have great faith in the power of sheer will. I see the result of my passion to find you and bring you home. It looks like I've created what I wished for and promised Nana. We have found you!*

It was certainly smart and clever of you to arrange for a numbered and noticeable piece to be spotted by HG in a field in Elsnig. Tomorrow when we go there, you won't be alone ever again. I can touch the soil where you are buried and pick the flowers that grow there—flowers that are used to make oil. My mind is filled with gratitude for HG who dedicates his life to finding crashed warplanes and pilots who never meet their daughters.

The next morning, we drove eight kilometers to the village of Elsnig. As we turned onto a narrow road bordered by fields of sunflowers and traversed by the railroad tracks of an abandoned railroad station, everything was exactly as I expected it to be— oddly familiar but with dreamy, blurry edges. Despite all the evidence that would prove the myriad connections between field and pilot, I knew this was the place where we would find him.

Because a possible human bone fragment was also found, Hans-Guenther contacted the Joint POW/MIA Accounting Command (JPAC) through Landstuhl Regional Medical Center (LRMC), the largest overseas military hospital operated by the United States Army and the Department of Defense. Two mortuary officers were on their way to Elsnig. They would assess the field and collect the artifacts and possible human remains. Their assessment would either interest JPAC or not.

"All" I had to do was to get JPAC, which includes the Central Identification Lab in Hawaii (known now as DPAA: Defense POW/MIA Accounting Agency), to agree to excavate the field. I was already counting on JPAC's mission, "Leave No One Behind," to give me courage to ask.

Each year, JPAC sends recovery teams all over the world to former war zones in search of those left behind. As of this writing, there are still 79,000 missing from WWII. Only a fraction of them will come home, but not for JPAC's lack of interest, efforts, or dedication. It would only be two more years before a JPAC team of an anthropologist/archaeologist, an ordinance officer, three mortuary affairs officers, an Air Force photographer, a medic, a senior military officer who was the team leader, and one pilot's daughter would walk onto that field to reclaim my father and his P-38J Lightning. The unchanged field looked exactly as it did the day my father's plane flew over it in 1945. More than four decades of Russian occupation had frozen East Germany in time. I could only wonder what I would have done if the crash site had become a parking structure or an airport.

Until the Berlin Wall came down in 1989, development and progress were mostly nonexistent, and people of East Germany experienced only scarcity. They owned nothing but what was given them by the Russian government. Cars were acquired through a confusing political system that required a 15-year wait for delivery of a Russian-issued green car without bumpers or chrome. Citizens remained vigilant to basic safety and survival while poverty kept them laboring in the government-owned fields.

Thus, in 1989, the former East Germany began the prolonged march toward recovery and reintegration within their divided country. Though divided, the charm and kindness of its people remain evident. Elsnig, where the field lies, is the antithesis of Frankfurt. This lack of progress and retained simple existence provided me a view of history. It was, in the end, fortuitous that he crashed in this pristine place if he was to be found and the pieces of the puzzle assembled.

The field was still owned by descendants of the original owners in 1945. Manfred Thiel, one of the crash eyewitnesses on Friday, April 13, 1945, married Traudl Bormann, the daughter of the original field owner. Though we were there to tear up their field in a most deliberate way, we were graciously accommodated on and off the field. JPAC paid for the crops lost to the excavation. In exchange, and just because the field owners were generous, we enjoyed many meals, music, and conversations at the Thiels' home.

When I mentioned that my father was Catholic, a lovely, oiled oak cross appeared at the field's edge under a tree. It sits directly parallel with the impact site where my father's few remains were eventually found. My heart was only beginning to fill with gratitude and love for the people of Elsnig. I had much to learn from them about war and peace, reparation and forgiveness, friendship and family.

As we stood together where my father died, Frau Thiel showed me a photograph of her father who was killed on April 18, 1944, in Slobozia-Ganeasa in Bessarabien at a Russian prisoner of war camp. Knowing that German prisoners experienced an 85 percent mortality rate in Russian camps, she believed he was buried in an unknown mass grave she would never find or visit. When she attends to the cross at my father's field, she also thinks of her father, Friedrich Wilhelm Bormann. She cannot travel to visit her father's grave, so we share this one. This is the generous spirit of the German people of Elsnig.

She said it would comfort her to care for my father's crash site grave as she would if it belonged to her father. Though our fathers were victims of opposing sides of the same war, they each have daughters who miss them. She called me her sister and placed flowers from her garden to honor her father and mine.

Ours was a friendship forged with empathic connection. She spoke no English, and I was dependent upon the kind translation of multilingual Germans, yet we understood each other fully. Our father-loss experience was our shared reality and interconnecting pieces of the same puzzle.

Wolfgang Günther was born on December 28, 1933, at Elsnig. He was 11 years old when, in April 1945, the following happened:

It is early afternoon, just after lunch (~13:00). Me and my father were on the way to our field to dibble potatoes. We just crossed a railroad embankment with our ox-drawn cart when German flak standing nearby at the railway opened fire (only a few shots). We immediately looked up and saw an aircraft that was hit and started to burn. It came down spinning. My father pulled me from the cart down below the railroad embankment into a waste pipe to take cover. We were just down in the pipe when we heard a big bang.

After this we went on with our ox-drawn cart to the scene of the crash. In 1945, the road called Butterstrasse that we were driving is just a sandy cast track. I remember clearly the crash site. We were the first to arrive, and we saw a torn-off arm with a wristwatch laying about two to three meters into the field near the ditch which runs along the road. Only a few remains of the aircraft were above the surface. The aircraft was burning fiercely, and ammunition was exploding. The heat did not allow us to go closer to the wreckage than 20 to 30 meters. Despite this we went around the crash site but saw nothing more of the pilot.

When coming back to the place where the arm was laying, I noted that the wristwatch was now missing. In the meantime, more people did arrive. The military police begins to cordon off the crash site. One wing and an engine of the aircraft were laying further away at the railroad embankment.

Manfred Thiel, born December 2, 1935, came to Elsnig from Berlin in February 1945 with his family. At first, he lived at 13 Dorfallee in the lower part of the village of Elsnig.

I was standing in our courtyard when I first heard a loud noise; then I saw several airplanes (I remember three to five) approaching from the direction of the village of Roitzsch. I assume that their altitude was only about 400 meters. The airplanes were flying line astern. Suddenly, there is a bang; the left wing of the first airplane breaks off, sailing upwards. At the same time, this airplane dives over the side of the missing wing and crashes. I saw no parachute. The other airplanes at once make a turn, flying back to the direction they came from. Afraid that the airplane might crash on me, I was running back into the house. After about two hours, I gathered my courage to visit the crash site. I walked to the field, meeting many people there. Today, I remember the site very well, which is situated near the road called Butterstrasse leading from Elsnig to Sueptitz. The field belongs to the Bormann family; later I married a daughter of that family.

I remember the airplane lying about three meters deep in the ground, with only the rear protruding by about half a meter above the ground. One wing and an engine were lying about forty meters off towards the village. I also remember a torn-off ring-finger lying about three to four meters from the impact point, and I have seen the imprint of a wedding ring on that finger but not any ring.

As well I remember an anti-aircraft gun-emplacement at the railway station from where the airplane was fired at. It was a railway anti-aircraft gun.

Eleven days after my birth and 12 days before my father was shot down over Elsnig, he was granted what was euphemistically called "flak leave," which was time off from battle fatigue. He professed to needing a rest more than he knew and hoped to return to war refreshed and renewed. While at a dance held at the rest facility, he met Pat Ellison, a young English wife and mother. My father wrote my mother a lengthy letter explaining the meeting, assuring her of his fidelity, and sharing with her the pleasure he received from this bit of normalcy in the midst of war. He asked her to post a photo of Pat with Susan in their scrapbook. No photo ever appeared, but the letter was saved among the others.

3/31/1945

Angel: Well, I'm really checked out on baby handling now. I gave Susan Ellison (age 15 months) her bath the other day, and even checked and changed her diapers a number of times. Even took her for a walk one fine afternoon, so our baby had better look out. Her mother and I met at one of our rest house dances. English girls are invited so our boys don't have to get out and scout around (or, as in my case, don't care to) for someone with which to dance. You, knowing how horrible my dancing is, can certainly understand my amazement when this young lady (who is the wife of a Royal Navy officer) didn't complain and grumble as I trampled her feet. I told her about you and our forthcoming wee one, showed her your picture and so on. Finally, she got a word in about her husband and child and did me one better by displaying a picture of both.

Honestly darlin', It was absolutely grand to talk to a girl who was so like you (except she didn't display or entertain your she-wolfish instincts). The dance was over at 1100, so I escorted her to the train and finally home. Her friend's mother, with whom they live, asked me to lunch for the next day. Had a simply grand meal! Am certain, tho', they used their entire meat ration for the one meal. The chops were over an inch thick.

Little Susan is a beautiful baby and such a happy little squirt. I asked to change her diapers to try my hand and did, if I do say so (blushing slightly), a marvelous job. Of course, her mother (whose name is Pat) had to hold her. She's such a squirmy little worm, I couldn't manage all alone. You gals just must have an extra arm that you keep concealed and use to hold babies for diaper changing and baths.

A couple of days later, I took Susan and another girl's baby out for a walk. Those kids have just been checked out on walking and ran the legs off me. One would go east and one south and so on. Anyway, I enjoyed it a lot.

I'd almost lost faith in human nature and European morals and all that. But, those visits to Pat's home and baby helped me out a lot. I owe her a debt of gratitude. She was a grand companion, and I am sure you'd like her because, as I've said, she's a lot like you and seems to agree with your opinions and ideas on everything. "Briefed" her quite thoroughly on your likes and dislikes, what you wear, and that sort of thing.

Honestly, these mothers do have a difficult time in securing the proper foods for their children. A baby only gets three fresh eggs per week and an orange (if mama is lucky and gets to the store when they have such things). Also, all the children's clothing is rationed; **even** *diapers and* **shoes**, *which means the mother must give up her coupons to ensure the baby is properly clothed. Then, to add to it all, most of the things are utility models and don't really wear the way they should. Actually, I didn't hear either Pat or her friend grumble at all. These people have endless patience—and "queue," as they call it, for everything from busses to sardines.*

This is perhaps a wild letter, but she showed me how grand and good and true a wife can be and was proof that my resolve to save me for you and you alone was the wisest decision I have ever in my life made (except, of course, in loving you in the first place). I realize the great love I have for you by her good example alone, not to mention her grand personality and sense of humor (a lot like yours).

She gave me two pairs of baby shoes for you and a book of the fairy tale, "The Pied Piper of Hamlin," and actually apologized because she couldn't get anything else. You see, I had a couple of bars of Woodbury soap in my kit and took it out to her for the baby and herself. The only soap they get is quite harsh and even it is rationed, so she was tickled pink.

Managed to get a picture of her and Susan, wish you would put it in your scrapbook, for she was a literal tonic for me and is a good friend of yours, even though you've not met. She and the old lady have asked me to let them know about our baby, so if you'd like to send a note along describing the kid and so on, I'll forward it for you.

Sweetheart, I've gone into all this detail so you'll realize the benefit

I derived from knowing Pat and the way it's helped me, because I was dern well disgusted with the whole world and their loose (or absent) morals, their cockeyed outlook, and all that. Incidentally, I'm free to tell you now, I was as nervous as a cat, without realizing it, of course, but now am back to what I consider normalcy. I've even stopped having those crazy dreams, by the way.

Honestly and truly, she is the only gal I've met since leaving you and the only one I care to meet, by the way, for as I've said, she, with her fine example, strengthened my resolve to be yours alone.

All my love, sweetest, Gener. P.S. Guess you could actually sum up your whole opinion in one statement—that you did or did not put the picture in the scrapbook!! Love and kisses, G.

He never received my mother's response, which was tucked inside her next letter to him. It was returned to her as "casualty mail," but she was gracious and kind, offering her friendship and gratitude for their kindness to her husband.

4/11/1945

Dear Pat and Susan, I feel as though I know you both. Gene has written in great detail of his visit with you. Pat, I want to thank you for making his leave in England such a pleasant one. It is girls like yourself that make the waiting here at home ever so much easier. He sounds like he is really much the better for his leave. [She wrote in some detail about me, then three weeks old. My father would be killed two days later.] *I am enclosing this in a letter to Gene so will have to make this note brief. Hope you will let me hear from you one of these days. Thanks again for everything. Love, Mary and Sharon*

A PAUSE WITH PURPOSE
IN GEISSEN, GERMANY

With a lull between the discovery of what we believed to be my father's crash site and the pending excavation, I figured out a way to live in Germany for a while. As my usual luck and certain skills would have it, the Department of Defense hired me to work as a therapist on a US Army base in Giessen, former East Germany, very near the east–west border. Part of my job was to ease the passage of soldiers coming from and going to Iraq, giving them a venue in which to explore their feelings about what they experienced or most feared about going down range to the front lines of the Iraq War.

In a stroke of irony, I arrived at the base for my first day of work to learn that a young first lieutenant and Bronze Star recipient, Timothy Price, had been killed in Baghdad, Iraq, earlier that day. It was Tim's second tour of duty as a platoon leader when a sniper killed him as he secured a burning army vehicle. I was one of two therapists assigned to the base. Our responsibility was to help manage the grief, loss, and posttraumatic fallout from such catastrophic events. It became evident that Tim was a highly regarded officer whose death would define and elevate the work before us.

> *1st Lt. Timothy E. Price, leader of the 3rd Platoon, 127th MP Company, was killed in action in Baghdad, Iraq, on Tuesday, Sept. 7, 2004. At the time of his death, Tim was attempting to secure a defensive perimeter around a disabled Army vehicle that had been struck by an IED (Improvised Explosive Device) and was in flames. Tim, who was 25, was serving his second tour of duty in the Baghdad area.*

At the end of the first week, I stood in the base chapel's choir loft above the overflowing crowd of military and civilian mourners at First Lieutenant Tim Price's memorial service. As I watched each member of Tim's MP company walk toward his helmet, boots, and weapon for a final salute, I realized that the death of a loved one in war was a universal and timeless event. Even though I never knew Tim Price, his death and the death of my father are connected across the landscape of war. I wondered if, after September 11, 2001, our nation had gone into grief rather than war, we would be any closer to resolving our collective anxiety and fear. I thought about the burial for my father that my mother never had. I'd like to do that for us.

Tim's father, John Price, wrote of our shared experience:

> *I have dealt with the loss of my son in ways that make sense to me. My greatest motivation has been to preserve Tim's memory. As long as Tim is remembered, a part of him remains alive. The sniper who killed my son killed a part of me with that same bullet. My life will never be as rich as it was when Tim was alive, but at moments when I think I can't continue, I feel Tim's nudge. Although I know there won't be any new memories of things we planned to do, I wouldn't trade a single moment spent with*

my son. When asked if knowing Tim is worth the grief I feel at his loss, I never hesitate to say yes. I will be forever proud of the accomplishments of my warrior son who heeded the call to duty and gave his life for his beliefs.

A reflective letter written by my father late in 1944 echoes John Price's sentiments:

11/8/1944

My Guiding Star: I know I can go into combat unafraid because I've made my peace with God. I know that what I'm fighting for is right and decent, so I will be able (I pray) to do my job properly and with a conviction that it's the right thing. Think I'll be able to do a fair share, and still manage to get back, because I've such a wonderful wife to return to. But my dearest, if anything should happen, you know that it will be doing the thing I love best next to you. Actually darling, I'm never very far from you, and when I'm flying, I sometimes feel even nearer. So, my dear, I pray not so much for my safety, as for the strength and help to do my job, whatever it is, properly. Actually, honey, I know I'm just as good as any damn fighter pilot in the world, if not a little better, so don't worry about my ability. In addition, I'm flying the finest fighter ever designed so looks like an unbeatable combination from where I stand.

SPIEGEL TV AND WATCHFUL DAUGHTERING

We worked hard all week on the base, organizing discussion and processing groups for military personnel and spouses; having therapy sessions with whoever requested or were mandated to get mental health support; and working with the base commanders, senior officers, and chaplains as needed. It was a full and rich experience, sponsored by the US Department of Defense at a critical point in the early part of the Iraq war. It wasn't predictable or mundane. The opportunity to see war from the point of view of those who lived it was incomparable to anything I'd experienced or known. My role as a woman whose father died in a distant war wasn't the point. Yet I learned much from their lived experience, trials, and losses. I came from there with a deep pride and a new level of patriotism.

The other benefit was that two train rides from Giessen would take me to Torgau. From there, I was only a few kilometers away from Elsnig and my father's field. The excavation wasn't yet on the books, though Hans-Guenther and I remained hopeful. One weekend, I visited my Elsnig friends and Ernst, who came from the distant Eifel Mountains to be there. On the train, I wrote my father a letter, as trains are excellent for writing, reading, and ruminating.

Field Notes, 9/24/2004

Dear Gener,

This is where we find ourselves—such a curious circle, weaving its way through the days of my life. Nearly 60 years later, and today, I can easily travel toward all I have of you. The picture becomes very clear when I am with you in Elsnig. Today, Ernst met my train and drove me to your field. I am grateful for his wise company. We walked there, mindful of what might appear on the surface this time. Not soon enough, we will have the evidence we seek, and the circle will quietly close. You will be free to fly again. With love from your daughter.

In late 2003, word of the possible discovery of a lost WWII crash site reached the German media. When Kay Siering, a documentary producer for Spiegel TV in Hamburg, contacted us to ask if he could make a film about our search and recovery, we said YES. Since a documentary film was the imagined part of my father-quest, having experts step up to do it was an unexpected bonus. Kay Siering confirmed it in a letter.

Dear Dr. Taylor,

My name is Kay Siering, and I am editor of Spiegel Television, the TV department of the German news magazine Der Spiegel. Last week I met with Mr. Hans Günter Ploes who told me the story of your father's last flight in World War II. I think that this story is very interesting.

For our formats Spiegel TV Special (broadcast on VOX, 100 minutes) and Spiegel TV Themenabend (broadcast on VOX, 50 minutes) I would like to produce a high-quality documentary about the last flight of your father. For the film, we would like to cover all important parts of the plane and body's recovery and identification. Also, we would like to talk to you, your father's wingman (in the US), and the eyewitnesses of the crash (in Germany). Besides, we are searching for old photos, films, and documents about this special flight and your father's life. The result should be a very complex and detailed film.

My questions are: What do you think about the project in general? Are you interested in helping us produce such a documentary? If so, do you have any contacts to the recovery teams of JPAC (we need JPAC's authorization to shoot at the recovery and identification)?

Please find attached an English version of our corporate profile. For further information, please visit our websites www. spiegelgruppe.de or www.spiegeltv.de.

Thank you in advance for your help. I am looking forward to hearing from you soon.

Best wishes,

Kay Siering
Spiegel TV
Editor

THE EXCAVATION
OF LIEUTENANT
ESTILL'S FIELD

W hen I saw the field for the first time in March 2003, it was a simple, functional growing field that, though forever changed on Friday, April 13, 1945, remains the same. By the time I arrived there in 2005, excavation preparations were underway, and the field no longer looks pristine. It is easy to see that the field has remained exactly as it was 60 years ago when a squadron of American fighter planes flew overhead en route to their home airfield.

During the war, anti-aircraft guns traveled the railroad tracks searching for enemy aircraft. On the day my father's squadron flew over the field in Elsnig, a waiting gunner tracked his plane from the tracks below. The field and the tracks stand as they were then, only one still productive, the other abandoned— both haunting and ghostly.

12/28/1944

Had a strange dream last nite. It seems that I rolled over in my bed and noticed the mattress had a rather strange, fluffy, white appearance. It developed that I imagined myself sleeping on a mattress comprised of 20-millimeter flak bursts. It was the same snowy white puff encircling a dull red flash that a fellow sees when one is close. Why the bloomin' thing even popped faintly, the way it sounds above the engines. Guess I'm nutz, huh?

On August 12, 2005, I received a press release from JPAC. In the past, I had read releases from JPAC with passing interest, always believing that one day the news would be about my father's recovery. It was a surprise to finally see him in the press release:

*Release No. 05-29 August 12, 2005. JPAC Teams Deploy to Europe Hickam, AFB, Hawaii - Two recovery teams and one investigative team from the Joint POW/MIA Accounting Command will deploy this week from Hawaii to conduct operations in five European countries to search for or bring home remains of Americans still missing from World War II. The first recovery team will deploy to Germany to conduct recovery operations East of Torgau, Germany and North of Hanover, Germany at two sites. **One site is associated with a 1945 loss of a P-38J aircraft,** while another is associated with a 1944 loss of a P-51D aircraft.*

A single sentence carried with it the implications of war across time and included the grief of a young widow, a mother, a father, a younger brother and sister, and a daughter who would make it her business to bring her father home from the war.

I was proud of my father's sacrifice despite my lingering fantasy that he would show up one day. I often wondered if my mother would choose her husband—my adopted daddy—or my father. When I'd actually be foolish enough to ask her who she would choose, she'd give me a "look," and no amount of insistence would result in an answer. Still, I liked to think of us being flown into our new life by my father.

The fact is that when I stood at the crash site for the first time, and the evidence was pretty clear that this was where he died, my fantasy died. I've spoken to many men and women whose fathers never returned from WWII, and they report the same hidden dreams that maybe their dads aren't really dead. Not difficult to understand considering the absence of evidence for many of us. In lieu of waiting for my father's return, I would bring him home another way.

However, the beginning of the journey was anything but auspicious. My departure into the unknown world of crash site excavations, anthropology, munitions experts, archaeology, grids, and sifting was completely unfamiliar to me. As I journeyed to Germany, I wondered about the degree of involvement I would be allowed and if I would have to fight for the rest. So many unknowns. Sometimes, the best stuff happens in the midst of walking toward it rather than anticipating everything in advance. I expected that the people who were coming to my father's crash site would be nothing less than professional experts accustomed to doing what I regard as a holy epic. It was I who would be impressed and awed and grateful. It was a rare opportunity to bear witness while the earth in which my father's bones lay was turned stone for stone to bring him to the surface.

Everyone wanted parts: The Germans wanted the plane parts, JPAC wanted the body parts, and I wanted everything. Any found bones would be on loan to JPAC, as they would eventually be returned to me. I represented my father in this deal. My mother might do it if she were there, but this was left to me to carry through to the end and not worry about how I got there.

I had seen a few airplane pieces by now. I owned some, and I planned to have more on my return trip. One was a stack of thinly sliced, faintly aqua or watery blue Plexiglas. Three layers made a windscreen tinted to reduce glare. It was amazing that it remained for us to see and wonder about its fortitude and why one fragment survived but not another. It was a piece that would make a fine, eclectic sculpture along with the buckle, the valves and pistons, and regulators from the cockpit control panel.

Then there was the business about the severed arm and hand, a watch, a wedding ring—there one day, gone the next. It was wartime, I rationalized, belying the truth that I'd love to have his watch. I was left to wonder but not yet to ask what became of my father's arm and hand—his left arm and left hand, hence the wedding ring. Were they buried or thrown on a trash pile somewhere or ditched like the terrifying representatives of war that they must have been?

Instead of knowing the comfort of his arms and hands, of feeling his fingers wipe away tears and teach me to tie my shoes, I was ruminating about the disposition of those items in a most literal way. I have his writing, and I can do his signature as well as he could if I take my time and think while writing with a fountain pen: Shannon E. Estill. He wrote mostly in cursive style in perfect Palmer penmanship, for which he received an award in grade school.

Despite the awful reality and consequence of my father's demise, I have received many gifts as a result of my status as the daughter of a father killed in war. I have had a solitary purpose for most of my life to know more about him and to know for sure that he loved me as much as I wanted it to be true. We are the classic unrequited love story—we never even laid similar colored eyes on each other, yet he is the love of my life.

I considered myself tenacious, brave, and fearless—and, sometimes, astute and competent. I would do whatever it took to get my father-loss issue resolved. I was the caretaker of my father's remaining existence. As long as he was buried in a field in Germany, it was my job to change that.

Ernst and I had discussed the possibility that my father was at peace in the Elsnig field and that I was disrupting his actual resting place. Would he object to being displaced, or was it the romantic mission I envisioned? A daughter bringing her father home to be buried on native soil among his fellow fallen soldiers, sailors, and fighter pilots could not be denied. I had the right and the obligation to do this with the blessing of the world.

If I was to walk my walk as well as talk, I could say that the purpose of this hiatus from real life would eventually be revealed. I couldn't then anticipate what I was supposed to do or what I would be doing once this was behind me. My intention was to document my father-quest without exploiting my father or myself.

That was my greatest hesitation in taking this to the media. The story begged to be told as universal and resounding in romance and intrigue. The core of it lies in my parents' letters, of course. The power of those words on the page is stunning. As I read my father's last letters again, I realized my father was a joyous man, and joyous men are in short supply.

It would be best if no one attempted to "protect" my sensibilities or keep anything from me. I wanted to know, see, and touch whatever came up from the earth. I wanted to hold my father's bones in my hands and be grateful for the accessible earth that held them for so long and with such certainty that I would come for them one day.

On August 17, 2005, after a delayed takeoff from Heathrow, I was finally on my way to Germany via Munich, which I hadn't visited since 1972. The driver who took me from the hotel to the airport that morning asked why I was in Germany and then if I had a website. He reminded me that this story was interesting enough to publish. I told him it was a novel idea for me to be so forthcoming with my life in this manner.

In those days, everyone who knew of my purpose passed it along to someone else. We've come into a technological future world, and the sweet simplicity of the handwritten word is passé, even though my parents' letters are the catalyst that brought me to this quest. My father emerges from his words in a way that can only be true inspiration. I actually feel his presence when I read his letters written to my mother—I no longer feel like the voyeur I did at the start. Instead, I believe his words are intended for me, and that was the point when he wrote them. On a mortal level, he couldn't know that, I suppose, but I don't rule out the "knowing" on some level. He was, after all, in the process of leaving me a legacy. I had been bequeathed a treasure map—a code to be deciphered by a daughter.

4/12/1945, His Last Letter

*Sweethearts: At last the mail is coming through again, so I'm as happy as a bug in a rug. Simply amazing how a note from you two makes me feel. Besides, they're so clever that I guess I'd enjoy them even if they were addressed to someone else. (Of course, **if** they were addressed to some fortunate fellow other than me, I'd be forced to clobber him and have you for my own, ok?)*

Here is a picture of the rest house. About a hundred yards to the rear was the beach; one day, sitting out on the sand, I very nearly jumped in and swam over to you, but had that little baby with me, and didn't want to leave her alone.

Now angel, in view of all my experience with wee ones, I feel qualified to advise you in any problems that might arise concerning Sherrie, so don't hesitate to write me if you are confronted with any unusual problems. Just ask me, you see I'm a Pop myself!

A Pop myself! Can hardly realize the fact. Guess I would if I were there to change a few diapers, huh? Sister Carmel's note about the wee one I shall include. She agrees that Sherrie is an unusual child. How strange that ours should be so perfect! Honey, my only request is that you send me a moose amount of pictures of my girls together. Now, be nize, beebees, and do dat, huh? Surely you can't expect me to believe I was baptized in a **dress***. Have always understood that my Christening outfit consisted of a cutaway and striped trousers.*

Read in a more or less recent issue of Life that women still favor manish clothing and couldn't help but recall how you wore my coat and pork pie hat that wonderful afternoon. Seems that I plied you with Hershey bars that day too. What a lover, huh?

Even that day, darlin', it seemed as tho' I'd known you for a long, long time. Wonderful days, darlin'. Even if we'd parted after a week or so, I'm sure I'd still remember you as clearly as now. You just stole my heart completely and never returned it. A fact for which I'm so thankful. Sweetie, guess I just love you too dern much! Egad! Almost midnite. Best get into my poor, lonely sack. All my love, you two, Gener

The letters that include reference to baby-me are particularly poignant. I remember how sad I was to read my mother's journal, after she died, in a futile search for any mention of me. When she did, it was in passing, as though I had an uncertain place in her life, as though her issues with the other three kids superseded any feelings she had about me. She told me once when she knew she was dying that she wasn't worried about me, as I was "settled" with a family and a husband. I would have loved a final letter from her, but it was not to be.

Letters and journals remain for me, as with my father, the certain way to preserve a thought and express a feeling. Words come easily to me, especially in writing. I remain a letter writer, as though it is part of my DNA. My father even wrote letters about writing letters:

1/28/1945

My own very dearest: Should have attended the group party tonight but instead succumbed to the temptations of my recently acquired books. Chose M. L. Shuster's Treasury of the World's Great Letters, which, needless to say, I find very engrossing; for, as the editor remarks, "Letters make the most interesting reading in the world—especially other peoples'."

TORGAU, ELSNIG, AND A STOPPED-CLOCK METAPHOR

O n August 17, 2005, Ernst and I traveled to the field and then over to the abandoned Elsnig train station. It felt like an integral part of the ritual of visiting my father's field. We stopped first at the field, which was resplendent in grass rather than crops and grooves of dirt. The next season hadn't been seeded yet due to the excavation. Thus, the field was splendid in a whole new outfit, unlike prior visits. It was peaceful and sunny in the late afternoon sun. It seemed like the field "knew" and was innocently waiting. It had a huge, silver bird crash into it, rendering it worthless for a while and probably injuring the integrity of its production that lean season. And then there was the matter of the body that lay beneath.

For me, the field carried an aura of something holy and divine. For the farmer, it was a day at work. It looked larger than I remembered. My illusion was entirely brought on by the change of season and the realization that JPAC must choose where they would begin.

The centerpiece for me was the train station clock, where the gunner waited. I noticed "Elznig" painted in old German writing. On either side of the station, I anticipated seeing the big clock stopped at a little before 1200 on the trackside of the building, but it had been taken away. When I saw it in 2003, I knew it was a powerful omen. Clocks have been a constant with the Estills. So, when it was missing, I felt a sense of loss—for the clock and for me. Ernst says everything changes. Yet this place never seemed to move toward change. The field was then as it was decades before, and the clock was there when it happened. Now it's gone—perhaps a small thing, but an indicator of forward motion: the fragile treasure of this field.

August 18, 2005, was our first day at the Elsnig field. Ernst told me the JPAC team was a bit reticent about the media attention, but we knew the kindness of the local people would override that. The fact that I was present would also impact things in a new way for the team. When the team leader called, he said they were "honored" to have me there. I was pleased and relieved, and I took it as an intention on their part that I could incorporate my presence there.

The majority of the day's work was devoted to survey and GPS. They needed to determine the space in which they would work and my role in the process. Captain Emmons called to tell me he was going out for permits, and then the team would gather at the field. He directed me to Dr. Greg Fox, the archaeologist/anthropologist, to determine how I could participate. This was where I hoped to prove my worth, not only as an interested relative, but as a contributing team worker. As the clock started that day on the excavation of the Elsnig field, it would take on a life of its own.

My best shot at being part of this was to be present when they were and willing to do anything. I wondered if the team noticed the energy change in the field. The day before, it was green and unturned, readying for new crops. Now it would be interrupted until our work was finished.

The work was incomparable. It was as I imagined it would be; yet, as I arrived at the field, I was overwhelmed by the reality of the marker flags, the equipment, the busy team, and the purpose of their industry. The day's work was informed and organized, deductive guesswork—preparing for the excavation so the digging could be purposeful. I was told that this preliminary work was tedious but necessary to the final outcome of the excavation.

Captain Emmons told me they sometimes hired guards for excavation sites to avoid any interference by relic hunters. Since this was a gravesite, the accuracy of preliminary work was important to the final success of the excavation. It wouldn't do to have outsiders mucking around in the field, no matter how fascinating it had become.

From what I could see of the archaeological strategy thus far, it was a tedious and (hopefully) precise project. The intent was to locate the point of impact, perhaps three meters below the surface, in order to obtain the richest store of artifacts and remains.

When Ernst and I arrived at the field, an endless row of cars, vans, and bicycles were parked along Butterstrasse Road, and a television crew was in an adjacent field. Our field was already filled with fluttering little red and yellow flags, indicating metal beneath the surface. Nine team members, including an archaeologist, a munitions expert, a medic, several mortuary affairs guys, a photographer, a team leader, and others I had yet to identify, were busy measuring and setting flags. Everyone was military except the archaeologist, Dr. Fox. Captain Emmons had just returned from a difficult excavation in Vietnam.

The local media wanted stories and pictures, but only a few were authorized to interview the JPAC team. The Torgau paper was represented, as well as a television station from Dresden. Later in the afternoon, a *Morgen Post* reporter from Leipzig came by on his motorcycle to set up an interview for the next week. He looked determined and intriguing in his full helmet and leathers astride a very loud motorcycle. It was impossible not to notice his arrival among the staid, microphone/camera-wielding press that mostly arrived in vans and cars. His, we suspected, would be a different kind of interview.

It looked like a circus had arrived. Someone who was not a fan of our disruptive American business drove by and shouted for us to go home, but that was the exception rather than the rule. The Germans were, as they had always been on my previous visits, gracious and welcoming.

In the midst of it all, I viewed a collection of P-38 models crafted by local men and brought to the site for my inspection. One was an arm-span wide and was used in remote control plane competition. The other was tiny and perfect with authentic markings. The impact of my father's plane is far reaching.

Ernst and I were looking forward to our traditional visit with the Thiels. Frau Thiel's family has always owned the field where my father died, and it was her generous custom to invite us for what the Germans call "afternoon coffee." She put out coffee, tea (for me), and lovely cakes.

As I left the field late that afternoon, hundreds of tiny flags were flying in a light breeze like a field of hopeful tulips. Surrounding the field was ominous yellow and black tape posted with warning signs: *Betreten der Baustelle verboten! Eltern haften für ihre Kinder!* (Entering the banned site! Parents are responsible for their children!)

So it began. There was talk of sifting and sorting and evaluating. Some plane parts had already emerged, along with some bomb fragments and a tractor spring. Most of the stuff being sifted thus far indicated whether it was worth digging under the little flag. My goal in all of this was to be allowed to help. It was the only way I could feel useful and ask more questions.

Field Notes, 8/18/2005—*Today was amazing on many levels. I almost lost my ability to think and breathe when I first approached the field this morning and saw those little marker flags. This is a reality of which I am fully aware and welcome with open heart and mind. But to see the flags and to know what lies beneath took a moment to comprehend. I hesitated to walk there at first, though I've been all over the field before with less hesitation. This afternoon, when someone cavalierly suggested putting up a volleyball net, I knew the reality was all mine. This is simply a job for them, and my job is to make them aware of the person they seek in the dust.*

A CONFLICT AND
A CONNECTION

On the second day, progress was brief. The day began with the glorious and impressive construction of two pieces of sifting equipment resembling backyard swing sets, hung with square sieves made of mesh wire and plywood fastened to four canvas straps instead of swings and slides. The screens swung freely, and as the dirt was shoveled from the carefully calculated and well-placed survey trenches, it was sifted and evaluated. We hauled buckets from the blue tarp where the dirt was dumped from wheelbarrows in a process that awakened in me the strong desire to be the wiry little girl I was in 1957 when I received my first typewriter. She was strong and resilient and impervious to being outside for the entire day. My 1950s dream of becoming a foreign correspondent was laughingly coming true. My mother insisted that I wrote well enough to become a journalist. There must have been that potential adventurous air about me at seven and eight. Who knew?

It was one of those jobs where you must be wary of the sun but remain in it all day. Germans don't care about cold beverages as much as Americans do; there was no way to fill an ice chest or to keep water cold, so the work was hot, and we all talked about ice.

The rhythm of the digging, filling, sifting, sometimes saving what was sifted, and hauling buckets to be filled again consumed most of the morning. Ernst and a local man were measuring the perimeter of the area around the crash site against the measurements in a 1945 aerial photograph of the impact zone taken three days after the crash. There was much discussion about oblique distortion and of the true location of the original dirt road.

At midday, Ernst and I headed back to town to arrange for dinner with the team at the oldest Italian restaurant in Torgau. We stopped at a small bratwurst shop downtown for lunch, bought some warm, nonfizzy mineral water, and headed back to the site. The afternoon was devoted to trench digging, which would enable the team to find the crash crater—the reason we were there. Everyone dug, and no one complained, but the medic promised 800 milligrams of Motrin all around at the end of the day—he called it "vitamin M."

I photographed the evolving landscape and asked everyone questions. They were patient with me, and we could sense the suspense building with every shovelful of dirt. At 1600, the equipment was packed into trucks that had to be stored overnight at a former munitions factory visible from the field. I reminded everyone of the time and place to meet for dinner.

Ernst and I got into his car and noticed a truck barreling down Butterstrasse Road. The driver signaled Ernst that he wanted to speak with him. Ernst, ever the diplomat, asked the man how he could be of help. We were accustomed, by this time, to crowds of onlookers, most with cameras, and all encouraging and anxious for information. The driver, whose name was also Bormann—as in the original owners of the field—told Ernst that no one had his permission for us to be there. I noticed two things as I observed their interaction: Ernst looked concerned, and the wind picked up in an ominous way.

I apprised the team leader of the situation and suggested that he wait for a signal from Ernst before approaching the farmer. For nearly an hour, things looked grave. The team linguist approached them, and the farmer angrily waved him away. Finally, the discussion ended, and the farmer got back into his truck.

Ernst reported that he was the only owner who was, for some reason, not asked for permission to do what we had been doing for the past two days. A caveat, in retrospect, was that *if* JPAC had known about him and gone to him for permission, he may have refused. We will never know, of course, but what was clear was that Herr Bormann expressed the resentment of his ancestors for all the oppression his family had felt under Hitler, the Russians, and, of course, the arrogant Americans. Hence, he was denying permission for us to continue, and he would not be convinced otherwise. He did, however, agree to return to the field early the next day to meet with the team leader and Ernst.

This was not the spirit in which we'd hoped to enjoy our dinner that evening, though it became the sole topic of discussion and much speculation and outrageous responses.

After dinner, I returned to the hotel to write a letter, which I later asked Ernst to translate and give to the farmer on my behalf at or before our meeting. The truth was that I felt powerless, unable to speak for myself in the language he would understand, and fearful that my quest might end without answers. Add that to the fact that the advance team spent a week gathering all the permissions they thought necessary. Had a simple oversight brought such a devastating result? Was this a cosmic joke? A small photo of my smiling father stuck to the wall above the desk in my room provided no answers.

Through the realization and shock at the abrupt change of events, I sought to understand the farmer's historic and cellular resentments. I believed he thought of Americans as the enemy. What he was expressing in denying us permission to retrieve our dead pilot was his control over what had been centuries of abuse by powers far greater than his family and the lasting effect of a war. He had been kept in the dark about too many things to allow one more, so I decided to tell him my story.

It is a strange thing to realize how ironic life can be. Some days the dragon wins, but this wasn't one of them. There are a few heroes in this story. Among them, the Burgermeister of Elsnig, Herr Grossman; Ernst; JPAC's willingness to go to all lengths and make all amends; and the farmer-owners themselves. Burgermeister Grossman arranged a 1400 meeting for the team leader, the archaeologist, the linguist, Ernst, me, the farmers Bormann, and the kind Burgermeister. I had strict orders from JPAC that my letter was to be used only "in case of fire."

We gathered in the Burgermeister's office, where the Bormanns greeted us with little enthusiasm. The elder brother began speaking as Ernst translated, though the message was clear that they had no intention of granting us permission to excavate the field.

In the midst of the conversation, understood by half of us, Ernst took my translated letter from his inner pocket and glanced at me. He carefully unfolded the two pages. We knew we had reached a moment of critical mass that qualified as all measures possible. He had decided it was time to read the Bormann brothers my words.

Dear Herren Bormann:

I am writing to ask that you read this and allow me to beg your forgiveness on behalf of those who failed to seek and obtain your permission to excavate your field in order to find my father's body. Your anger is completely understandable to me, and though I had no part in this terrible oversight, I feel deeply responsible and saddened that it has caused you such anguish and discomfort. You do not deserve to feel this way.

This is not my first visit to Torgau, Elsnig, or Germany. I've traveled throughout Germany with Hans-Guenther Ploes, who knows where most WWII aircraft crash sites are located. This would be a solitary endeavor but for Hans-Guenther's expertise and Mr. Eberle's constant kindness. Searching for my father who was shot down by anti-aircraft fire on April 13, 1945, fell to me because no one from our government ever looked for him. For one reason, this part of Germany was closed to us, and for another, the war was over, and it was possible to simply say "killed in action" without actually finding the dead pilot. This was the circumstance of my family. I was three weeks old when my father was killed and left my mother, a very young, grieving widow who never fully recovered from my father's death.

This is my sixtieth year and the sixtieth year my father's body has been in your field. In March of 2003, the good German researchers determined that this was the place of my father's crash. This has been exhaustively documented, and I began asking the agency who digs there now to put my father's name on their list for excavation and recovery. It took every day of these past nearly three years to make that happen. I have written countless letters and had more telephone conversations, emails, and personal meetings than I can remember. Having the team here now is the fulfillment of a lifelong dream for me, and my heart will be broken if I must walk away now and leave my father behind.

I did this, Herr Bormann, because though I never met my father, it seemed like my daughter's duty to bring him home to be buried with his parents near their farm in Oklahoma, USA.

You have been offended, and I cannot undo what insensitive, inattentive people failed to do properly. What I can do is implore your kindness in considering allowing the completion of this careful excavation of my father's gravesite and allow the agency to restore your field to its normal state, minus the dead pilot in the field. It would mean everything to me, the pilot's daughter, and I would forever be grateful for your kind permission. So, please allow me to take my father home. This will be my last opportunity, and I cannot begin to say how healing it will be for me and for my family to do so.

My friend, Ernst Eberle, will translate this for you, but I would be happy to meet with you if that is your wish. I hope you can honor my simple request and that you can find it possible to allow me this comfort.

With deepest respect,

Sharon Estill Taylor

Even in German, his reading was powerful and moving. The brothers listened intently. Ernst reached the end, refolded the letter, and handed it to the brothers. He never took his eyes off the Bormann brothers, nor did I. They requested a private meeting with Ernst and the Burgermeister. We waited.

When they returned to the table, Ernst translated the Bormanns' decision to set aside their objections. They attributed their change of heart to what I'd written. They said it helped them to know the story behind the request. As the brothers looked directly at me for the first time and smiled, they said that JPAC could learn diplomacy from me.

The JPAC team offered profuse and sincere apologies for any offense taken and assured the owners their field would be properly restored. When we all shook hands, I wanted to hug the Bormanns but refrained from being quite that American in my relief and gratitude. They touched me with their willingness to hear my story. I connected with them in my willingness to hear theirs.

DISCOVERING
PUZZLE PIECES

The morning of August 21, 2005, the clouds threatened to continue raining but stopped and gave us blessed cloud cover for a few hours. While the JPAC team dug trenches in a grid, I sat in one of them, smoothing the bottom with a trowel, scooping the dirt in a bucket. All dirt was valuable until it was determined to be just dirt. The trench dirt was then tossed onto blue tarps surrounding the field until it was sifted. We had the usual onlookers, and Ernst was always gracious in meeting and greeting them. A kind soul brought a basket of beer, but this wasn't work that was best done with a warm cocktail.

We began finding some interesting parts in the morning, but the best stuff was discovered in the afternoon. As we found parts and pieces, and if they were not ordinance material (ammunition exploded or unexploded), everything was carefully placed in a black bucket for inspection by Dr. Fox, the archaeologist/ anthropologist/boss of us. It felt a bit like a treasure hunt with emotional attachment. Someone uncovered a large piece which even I could identify by the rivets in a row. In all its preserved 60-year-old glory, it was once part of the exterior of my father's plane.

We had lunch in the shade (growing narrow by noon). I was happily dirty, which reminded me of playing outside as a kid and stopping for a by-then flattened peanut butter and jelly on Wonder Bread. The late afternoon's work revealed a stash of parts in one trench that was interesting enough for another trench to be started across it. The field from the air must have looked like a Scrabble board. I would have loved to fly over it to see what my father's squadron saw that day in 1945, but I was busy on the ground.

Because the stuff we were finding in the extended trench looked like cockpit pieces, we all began sifting, leaving Dr. Fox to prepare the trench for careful excavation the next day. Six of us took over sifting screens, one of the guys loaded dirt into the screens from a wheelbarrow, and we separated the dirt from the rocks and ACS (i.e., aircraft shit). In nearly every shovelful of dirt, some small or medium-sized pieces emerged. Several small bones were found.

After digging 96 meters of trench, it was possible we were at the exact site of one engine and the cockpit. Dr. Fox and I sat on the edge of the last trench and examined the ACS. He looked each piece over and tossed it back into the bucket, telling me to take them if they looked interesting. Thus, I became the proud owner of another bucket completely filled with my father's plane and miscellaneous crockery. Among the pieces was one that I kept in my pocket most of the day. We thought it might be a toggle switch that would have been on the instrument panel—a switch my father would have touched. It is interesting what becomes meaningful in this business of recovering history.

The work resumed smoothly after our brief hiatus on Saturday, wherein we were all reminded how much we wanted to find my father. This was a great day of physical labor unlike anything I had ever experienced. The reward was to look at the transformed field at the day's end and to know the possibility of miracles, the value of sweating in the sun, and liking it.

Field Notes, 8/21/2005—*I have the feeling that I am living in an alternate reality. It could be the experience I am in the midst of that causes this oblique distortion. I spend every moment immersed in the moment, which is the only way to make sense of this experience; even then, it remains surreal.*

I never lose sight of the fact that my father died in this place—flat out, without a moment of warning or advantage. One moment thinking of home or his new baby, and the next, blown out of the sky. As I sift the dirt where he and his plane lie, I realize the enormity of the catastrophe. He and the plane are in pieces. It takes an act of true skill or intuition to determine what's real and what's rock. Most of it is rock. The real stuff fills buckets and then is discarded because it isn't actually my father made of bones and marrow and DNA that matches mine. If not for his making of me, I wouldn't be here feeling like a pinball machine of emotions, with a little steel ball careening around the corners of my mind.

I am deeply but satisfyingly tired, but I look forward to tomorrow with joy and anticipation. Tonight, I will wash everything I'm wearing in the bathroom sink and hang it to dry for two days. Every day, I wear a clean pair of cargo pants, a sleeveless T-shirt, another shirt over that that has been treated with SPF 40, and a bandana around my neck. I alternate four outfits for the duration. My lovely work shoes are green rubber gardening boots, and I wear work gloves and an Air Force blue Team Estill baseball cap that says "Pilot's Daughter" on the back. My father's squadron logo is on the front. We all wear them, including the Bormann brothers who stop by to help every day.

What we find is monumental yet incremental, if that makes sense. The methodology of excavation is incredible in every possibly imagined way. I will know something about archaeology when I am finished. While others from the current war are burying their sons and daughters, I am exhuming my father from another war.

The next day, we found plenty of ACS and some osseous material (bones), but the day passed without the exhilaration of the day before. I was far less exhausted because there was less heat. The main trench was beginning to beckon us with a "what lies beneath" outline of a crashed plane. There were huge, twisted hunks of wire and cables poking out of the ground. Powdery battery acid material was scattered around the surface, indicating a cache of aluminum below—lots of it. The team's fervent hope was that this was the area where the cockpit lay and not the back boom.

Mostly, I sifted and even found two bones to contribute to the bone bag. It's no surprise that the proportion of bones to ACS is balanced in favor of the airplane parts. My father was a significant but small part of this dig. The airplane dominated the scene, scattered far and beyond where anyone would ever look. Archaeologists in the distant future will find pieces of my father's plane and have meetings to speculate about its origin. Only historians will know of the great war in Europe in the 1940s, by then ancient history. There is no doubt in my mind that plenty of ACS will remain, less some of my father.

It was surreal work—going backward in time and piecing it together. It was scientific yet intuitive. I learned enough on my treks with Hans-Guenther to recognize a piece of aircraft skin or a valve. We found the connector to my father's headphones: just the little piece that we now call a "jack." It went into the special bag for the cockpit pieces. The cockpit was the pot of gold at the end of the double rainbow Hans-Guenther and I saw as we left Weimar three years before. All the parts that the German wreck hunters and I held so dear were inconsequential to the team, except as indicators. All the pieces that emerged from the sifting were tossed into buckets, looked over and licked (yes, licked) by Dr. Fox, and summarily tossed into a discard pile, as appropriate. Discard means nobody could have these pieces until the end of our dig. There was always a review of what may have looked worthless just in case it fit with something meaningful later. Hence the puzzle picture emerges.

On August 24, 2005, we uncovered the crater. My lingering memory of the day is the smell of the crater as it was revealed. It was filled with burned parts of the plane and, after 60 years, smelled strongly of something recently burned. Many of the parts we examined were chunks of molten metal. The screening process became more tedious. My new mantra, as seen on a bumper sticker, was this: "Normal ist das nicht—Normal is not this."

By the end of the day, the items discovered in the crash feature (i.e., nontransportable artifact of human behavior) included the following:

- Intake and exhaust valves
- Solenoid to trigger machine guns
- Engine generator from one engine
- Rocker boxes for valves
- Pieces of instrument panel and possibly one part from barometric instrument
- Gear pump for hydraulic or lubrication of engine
- Rubber hosing of various length and dimension
- Pieces of oxygen mask and hose
- Armor plate from front cockpit area near pilot's feet
- Back plate from machine gun with steel spring
- Pieces of leather and webbing
- Glass for altimeter

- Plexiglas
- 250-plus 50 mm and 20 mm ammunition rounds with some links
- Unburned fiberboard
- Gaskets from exhaust pipes
- Switches
- 30 cm bolts for engine
- Electric wires
- Gears with teeth

In examining the list, a few salient points emerged. In and of themselves, the parts listed were described accurately as determined by educated opinion, some speculation, and brazen guessing based on what had been seen and learned from the exhaustive study of a P-38 parts catalogue. My father and the pilots like him had to know their planes well enough to fix them, and my father enjoyed working on his own plane. The parts catalogs, which served us so well, were his plane bible.

Each day, I found a piece that spoke to me in a meaningful way. One day, it was a little, jagged, flat shard of Bakelite (pre-plastic used in the 1940s) which Hans-Guenther told me was from the instrument panel. He said it would definitely have been one of the last things my father looked at in his life.

As time expanded to include all that happened, along with a copious amount of discovery at the "crash feature," I became rooted in the moment. Paradoxical thinking is the requirement for having this make sense. There is no way, even with technology and adjustment to time and place, to do it with less complexity. Going backwards in time and piecing history together in this way is focused work. It's scientific and intuitive. It's emotional and factual. It's dissociative and concrete. It's joyous and devastating to find important stuff in the screens when each indicates the catastrophic method of my father's death.

The plane parts were from what my father called his "iron bird." To anyone else, it was scattered rubble. Though the engine parts were mottled with rust and corrosion, it was easy to imagine their former power. My adopted 474th Fighter Group dads who flew with my father would remember the definitive sound of two Allison engines. Some fighter pilots would say that is why they are deaf.

In my father's last letter to my mother, he lovingly mentions his plane and why he was flying a borrowed plane the next day:

> *Ham pulled my plane out today for inspections, so it rained cats and dogs all day. Even the heavens are displeased when the big iron bird is grounded, I guess.*

As I worked in my father's field, the guys from my father's squadron were with me. I swear I saw Bill Capron leaning against the fence telling a story about flying over France. I wondered what they would make of this if they were there and how they would feel about the parts and pieces we were exhuming. Part of the glamour of the P-38 was that it was a complex and mighty piece of machinery built to fly low and fast. The pilots were brave, smart, and competent.

On the field, we spoke of these pilots and their planes, and we saw both quite clearly as we worked. My father's plane was smashed into a million pieces, yet we thought of it as whole. Its mighty spirit lived on in each fragment and rivet we found, as did the pilots who survived him.

I moved between parts and being part of a documentary film. It was a far less daunting experience than expected due to the professionalism of the Spiegel TV team. They were easily integrated into our daily rhythms and were facile in their ability to be where the action was, which was copious. They did two days of filming in one day, and they would return within the week for more. We all enjoyed having them around, and Dr. Fox declared them "unobtrusive." That's like a Catholic receiving a blessing from the Pope.

The German way of making documentaries is not to emphasize the dramatic with big music and slow-motion action scenes but to create more of an historic, yet personal, film. I expected that the stories told by the people and the cameras were dramatic enough in this case.

As though I hadn't received enough presents, medic Rodney Acasio handed me a JPAC dog tag, saying, "Ma'am, I know you don't have your father's dog tags, so I want you to have this one." From the chain holding his military dog tags, he removed one that was inscribed with these words:

PEOPLE FIRST—MISSION ALWAYS
JPAC STANDARD
DO WHAT'S RIGHT
ALWAYS CARE THE MOST
OPERATE THE BEST
GET BETTER EVERY DAY

On the other side, it said,

"UNTIL THEY ARE HOME"
JPAC VALUES
COMMITMENT
INTEGRITY
RESPECT
COMPASSION
HONOR

This gift embodied the people who served on JPAC teams and lived the mission. To a person on my JPAC team, these beliefs and code of ethics were in evidence every day. How, I wondered, could there be any more bittersweet joy in this event for me?

AN AUSPICIOUS SUNDAY

On August 26, our work was stopped in the middle of a deluge that arrived around 1500. We were off the field by 1515 just as I finished my interview with Alexander Bischoff, the correspondent from *Morgenpost*. Before the rain, we were all part of the upcoming evening news as Sylvia Krause, a freelance journalist, photographed and interviewed the entire team. Local newspaper reporter Nico Wendt published an article in that day's edition of *The Torgauer* in which he invited anyone who might have acquired any of my father's personal possessions after the crash to anonymously leave them at the newspaper office. He wrote specifically about my father's missing pilot's watch and wedding ring seen by an eyewitness to the crash in 1945.

It occurred to me, a formerly devout Catholic girl, to pray to St. Anthony ("Tony, Tony, come around. Something's lost and can't be found.") or to wonder at my own sanity for having any hope that these items would be returned. One reporter shook his head in amazement that I would even consider this possible. I suggested that he glance out over the field and tell me what is impossible. I put great faith in the good people of the community. If those items still existed and the right person read the article, they would be returned to me. If not, I could live with the fact that an attempt was made and that a war was on.

The parts from the deepening crater were large and ominous. A piece of one of the engine mounts emerged, and after it was somewhat cleaned, Dr. Fox fit an engine piece around it perfectly. Rectangular, metal data plates, identifying the aircraft, would have been on the engines and an essential find.

Meanwhile, the collection of bone fragments grew, as did the importance of careful and tedious screening. It was imperative to stay vigilant and not discard anything questionable. There was much consulting about this.

My final gift of the day came from Chris McDermott, a JPAC historian and friend of Hans-Guenther's with whom I had corresponded for several years. He brought me his little thumb drive on which he had stored a file he shared with me entitled "14201 Deferred Search File." It contained surprising proof that another team, much like JPAC in composition and mission, was sent to Europe in the years following the war to search for crash sites and missing men. This was news to me, as our family was unaware of this effort. My mother told me that they heard rumors about this but nothing that would lead them to think a search had ever been conducted on my father's behalf. It seemed fitting and honorable that JPAC was there to finish the job. It is also important to mention that through the efforts of Hans-Guenther Ploes, JPAC knew where to dig.

On August 28, Spiegel TV film producer Kay Siering and his team arrived at the field. Kay and I had been working on this project together for nearly three years since he called to see if I would be interested in having Spiegel TV make a documentary film about my father's last flight. The day's filming was essential to the cohesiveness of the rest of the film. As it turned out, Spiegel TV arrived on an auspicious Sunday morning.

At exactly 1115, Dr. Fox was scraping and brushing the side of the crater between the engine parts and what he hoped was the cockpit when he slipped a small, flat, rectangular piece from the dirt, tapped it a few times, and jumped to his feet calling for Hans-Guenther. He held the single piece of evidence that unequivocally identified this crash site as that of my father. At last, the needle in the German haystack had been found: the crumpled but identifying engine data plate.

The numbers visible on the plate (considering fire, general destruction, and a 60-year hiatus in the dirt) exactly matched the numbers recorded in the Missing Air Crew Report (MACR). It was a great moment, which, like winning a clattering, noisy jackpot on a slot machine, caused everyone to gather around and watch for a while.

The discovery and recovery fates were good to us that day. Shortly after finding the engine data plate, the bottom frame of the canopy emerged with shards of glazing still intact. The shards, like so many of the pieces we found, were charred but recognizable. Fortunately, the canopy frame was made of stainless steel. It was easy to see its true indestructibility in the shine of this twisted but pristine remnant.

Despite the return of the summer heat, we worked all day, and most of us were interviewed by the documentary team. Dr. Fox was our leading man, along with his costar, Hans-Guenther. I took careful notes as Dr. Fox explained the process to Kay Siering, the Spiegel TV producer.

A status report from Dr. Fox regarding the excavation:

The crash materials are spread out over approximately 80 meters.

The dig was started with survey trenches one meter wide, and trench sites were chosen according to eyewitness testimony.

Fortunately, the first trench hit where one of the engines was found. The other engine fell across the field toward the adjacent road along with one wing.

The engine crater was excavated first, and the trench was expanded outward.

It is possible a wing or tail boom also fell into this crater. The engine went straight down into what is now the pit. (Inertia at work.)

Throughout this crater, 20mm incendiary explosive rounds are found, which probably "gang fired" at the point of impact causing this widespread catastrophic result. Even the protective armor plating in the plane was broken into pieces.

The excavation will continue in one-meter-wide segments, and work will cease in that square only when sterile soil is reached.

Even after the entire area of the engine and cockpit craters, digging will continue around the edges for remains, personal effects, and material evidence that may have been dragged away by the plow.

Dr. Fox routinely examined soil colors for what they revealed, as layers of dirt were removed in a methodical way. Soil was one of the standards by which he could judge color, consistency, and compactness. The soil was evaluated in descending layers: natural sand, burned soil, and, finally, the turquoise decomposed aluminum. The P-38 Lightning was fully loaded with aluminum. The soil in the field was layered in blue.

My ACS collection was enhanced by three new discoveries: The gun camera emerged from the dirt with film still intact around the edges of what was the lens. Small gears remained visible on both sides. Those parts, though badly decomposed, made it a camera rather than a lug nut. We also discovered the oxygen flow indicator, a part of the instrument panel that allowed my father to see that oxygen was flowing into his mask. I added these to a large, fragile piece of the windscreen in which three layers of varying shades of blue Plexiglas were still visible. It was shattered but held within the framework of some of the windscreen.

If the devil is in the details, I probably missed a few, but it was a great way to spend a Sunday. We gathered enough evidence to ascertain that we were bringing home the right guy. I never doubted it based on Hans-Guenther's exhaustive research and intuition, but hard evidence beats conjecture, wishing, and hoping.

A quote from Hans-Guenther upon discovery of the engine data plate: "A wish is the father of the thought." This was our wish. This is what he knew and waited patiently to be proven.

THE FINAL DAY

August 29, I learned, was the last day we would search for my father's remains. A reporter told me Dr. Fox felt JPAC had made a good-faith effort, and he was pleased that we had uncovered key information from what remained in the crater.

I had been thinking about the parts and pieces that may have become wartime bounty left in the field. That could have included everything from my father's watch, ring, and other personal stuff that was flung far and wide to the metal and hinges of his plane. Some things may have meant survival for someone or their family in ways I can only imagine. He went beyond donating his life for his country. Circuitously, his death benefited those who killed him.

It would be difficult to witness the restoration of the field. I loved the energy we created in those weeks—the sheer effort and willingness to do this job for me and for my father. He must have been watching and smiling at us, because we were very lucky in what we found, and each thing had significance as a tiny surviving clue that allowed us to bring him home.

Dr. Fox and I sat at the edge of the crater for our last meeting. He showed me his hand-drawn maps and diagrams. They were the opposite of him in appearance. They were tiny and precise and immaculate in their presentation. He was unkempt, to say the least, but endearing to say the most. He walked me through the things he'd documented and told me that it was possible that more remains were still in the field. He said it wouldn't help us any more to blindly search for these stray parts, which may or may not exist—that we had enough to determine that this was my father's crash site. He also said that a part of my father will always be here. My father owns a little bit of Germany, and Germany owns him. At that moment, I loved that messy, jaded, clever, and irreverent man I'd watched for hours and days do the work of this recovery.

My father will always be here, and if people who come after this want to know about the cross in the field, now there will be answers.

As it all unfolded before me, I had moments of true revelation and sheer exhaustion. As I watched the crater unveil itself and morph into a visible shape of a P-38, I felt it as though I saw it land there. The picture appeared to me as a lens is focused to exact clarity. I'll never know for sure if he died in the air or on the ground—if he was frightened or just busy trying to right his plane. I know what I choose to believe, and that is what I will keep as my truth.

But for the final restoration of the field, the excavation was complete. Our work that day was significant and conclusive. After finding the main data plate and, with it, the confirmation that it was my father's crash site, all that remained was to complete the excavation of the two engine craters and the cockpit crater. The imprint of the plane, how it fell, and to what extent it was buried and, in all probability, dug up for its valued metal after the war were clearly evident in the soil.

Over the course of this quest, I kept the body bag in my mind securely closed. Now it was open, and there were few illusions left. What remained of my father wasn't anything I should have had to see or handle.

I had so little of him but for his watchful protection and certain love. I did the most intimate thing I could for him, and it was time to gather it up and do as I promised I would do.

"Nana, I am bringing him home."

WHAT REMAINS

On August 30, 2005, JPAC went to the field to deconstruct the screening equipment, to sweep and photograph the crash feature, and to arrange for it to be refilled with its own dirt minus the treasure we had claimed. I expected the day to contain a bittersweet center surrounded by an elusive sense of accomplishment, wrapped in the absence of action. It was the latter I dreaded most.

As usual, Ernst took me to the field around 0900 for one last look at the crater that contained so much, but in the end, offered only a small measure of its worth. As I stood there for the last time at the edge of the place where my father died, I wanted to fly above to see the ghostly image of a P-38 Lightning. My father's fighter group uses that exact image on their newsletter. It is indelible for me now in its symbolic and concrete message.

Standing on the field watching the evidence of the excavation disappear, I wondered how it could possibly be finished. This field was a metaphor for my search for my father. Once found,

I placed beneath its landscape my hopes and dreams of finding my father. Now, 60 years of questions were being plowed under and smoothed over in this final, essential, and promised work.

Just when I thought it was my duty to watch this final restoration to the bitter end, Hans-Guenther appeared at my side. He was wearing a tie with his special airplane tie tack, normally reserved for press events. He invited me to spend the day with him exploring Dresden and Meissen. Meissen is home to the oldest pottery manufacturing plant in Germany. I remembered the shard of pottery stamped with the crossed swords mark of Meissen found in one of the sifting screens.

Inspired by the final moments of seeing the crater as it would never be seen again, we left for our overland excursion. HG brought our usual provisions for the trip, including a huge bag of gummy bears and his collection of Beatles music.

With a backward look at the green farming machines restoring my father's field, I asked, "What went away from the plane as it crashed?"

Hans-Guenther's considered opinion was that the plane was probably spinning toward the earth. Spinning can be, as one might imagine, described in infinite ways. As it applies in this case, it was at an unknown speed at either a steep or flat angle. The plane was most likely hit by anti-aircraft fire just over where it landed. It looked to the trained eye (not mine) like the speed of the spin determined the shallow depth of the crater. Most of the damage happened at the point of impact and as a result of the subsequent fire due to stored ammunition and fuel supply.

The sheared-off front landing gear, which we found during the excavation, was found between the engine and cockpit craters and was not moved after the crash. This *may* mean that the airplane landed right side up. If it were the other way, the front wheel landing gear would have been on top and probably salvaged for its valuable steel.

The question of what actually fell away from the plane as it spun to earth remains a mystery. Hans-Guenther believes that there may be another six-by-four-meter hole containing these missing parts near the adjacent road at the other side of the field. This was where one of the engines was supposedly found, but the crater we excavated shows evidence of both engines landing there. A part of one or both engines, which measured one-and-a-half meters, would have protruded from the ground. This calculation was based on the depth of the crater and the known circumference of the engines. The farmer took those parts away so he could continue his plowing.

Both ailerons were found in the crater, plus the counterbalance weights that were attached to the wing tips. One of these lead weights was our first discovery in 2003. No main landing gear was found, which logically should have been present along with the rest of the plane, nor were the superchargers, or most of the cockpit along with what it contained.

The six-by-four hole may have been a repository for anything that didn't bury itself in the crash, including human remains. No remaining witness to its existence has come forward.

When Dr. Fox and I held our last meeting at the crater's edge late Monday afternoon, we discussed the rumor that airplane parts and remains had been buried along the boundary fence two weeks after the crash. Possible, he said, but improbable. A decision was made not to explore that area because enough had been gathered from the existing site to prove, beyond a doubt, that this was the place where my father's plane crashed on Friday, April 13, 1945. He said the amount of material taken from the site was estimated at one-half ton, give or take a few kilograms.

Hans-Guenther believed that nothing additional was thrown back into the main crater, undisturbed for the past 60 years but for occasional relic hunters. One variation on this theme was that two machine guns from the plane were dug up in the late 1940s and handed over to unknown American officials. He assured me that speculation and rumor always emerge around crash sites and that facts are only determined through excavation. He felt that a full and complete job was done by JPAC in the found crater. He also said he would bring his best deep-penetration detector to the scene "just for a look." Years later, Hans-Guenther, Wally Busch, and Ulf Podbielski returned to the Elsnig field to search the rumored field grave but found no evidence of human remains or aircraft parts.

There may be more than one hundred P-38 crash sites remaining in Germany. Only a few are associated with MIA pilots. Many of the pilots bailed out and were either rescued or lost but are no longer with their plane as my father had been.

"Possible" and "maybe" are often used to report this kind of ambiguous loss. This is the practice of highly educated deduction along with intuitive guessing, in conjunction with sorting and filing of accounts that may *possibly* be skewed after six decades of recollection and telling. The crater evidence is irrefutable.

My conclusive feelings, since every reporter in Germany likes to ask, are these: At the end of the war, when my father's plane crashed in this field, it provided valuable metals and materials that included what was left of my father's possessions, if anything could have survived. He would have wanted something useful to come of this catastrophe. He would have encouraged people to take what they needed for sustenance in a country without an economy at the end of a war. I like to believe that the retrieved pieces of his plane were recycled and made valuable again in some way we cannot imagine. Even if his watch and ring were taken from the crash site for whatever reason, my father would want that. Thus are the spoils of war and collateral damage commingled with the belief that *all is fair* in love and war.

I didn't know my father from seeing his face, touching his hand, looking into his eyes, or hearing him laugh. I know from the letters, from his constant presence in my life, through my children, his grandchildren and great grandchildren, his parents, his sister and brother and their children, and, of course, through my mother. He would have handed out every part of himself and his plane in order to ease the suffering of others and to do the next right thing. That's the truth.

Was I sad because the search, excavation, and recovery were finished? Even if a possible second or third site remained, our work was done. The inventory of found parts accounts for my father. If there was more, it didn't discount the inherent value of what the JPAC team brought up for us.

Was I satisfied? Yes. Did this change anything for me? It inspired me to fully consider things and people as even more fascinating and complex. My father's field taught me that what we see on the surface is nothing compared to what lies beneath. And then, it is up to us to determine how what is found is valued. I valued every tiny fragment of this grand challenge.

GALLERY 3
EXCAVATION

Team Estill in the field

Words above the Buchenwald Concentration Camp entry gate

Y-9 airstrip, 1945

Y-9 airstrip, 2003

Butterstrasse Road, Elsnig

Elsnig train station clock

Handmade cross in Lt. Estill's field

Herr Bormann, Ernst, and Bormann's dog

Traudl Thiel with her father

Hans-Guenther looking out over the Elbe River in Dresden

Headline in the Morgen Post

Data plate matching the missing air crew report

Aerial view of the crash feature at Lt. Estill's field

Part of a day's worth of ACS

Dr. Fox being interviewed by media

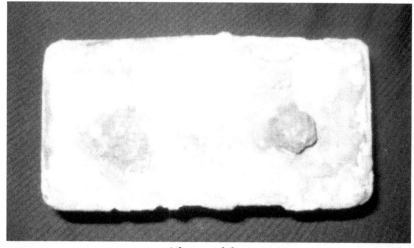

Aileron stabilizer

First found parts from Lt. Estill's plane

Pilot's seat harness worn by Lt. Estill

Instrument panel switches

Entry gate to Château le Beauchêne

German 88 mm FLAK 36/37 anti-aircraft gun

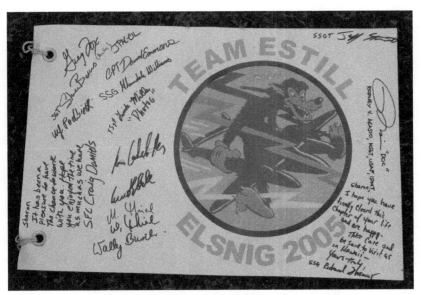

Signed flag that flew over the field during the excavation

THE BOMBER WITH
THE BABY SHOE
RETURNS HOME

On September 1, 2005, "The Bomber with the Baby Shoe" was the headline of an article about the excavation written by Alexander Bischoff for *Morgen Post*. During our interview, I told him the baby shoe story written in my father's last letter after he had just learned of my birth.

4/12/1945

As soon as the cable came about our daughter's birth, I took her little shoe out of the celluloid frame and tied it to the back of my helmet. Have carried it in my jacket pocket since my 10th mission and on the helmet since the 28th (I have 34 now). That is the cutest little boot—I'd love to see her in a pair just like it. You just stole my heart completely and never returned it, a fact for which I am so thankful. Sweetie, I guess I just love you too much. All my love to you TWO! Gener

4/8/1945, Birth Announcement

Little sweeties: I'll bet you two are having a grand time. Even tho' you are far, far away, I sometimes feel I'm with you, almost in the same room. Even feel as tho' I've actually seen Sherrie: just how, I can't explain. Guess my love for her Mommie is so great, I just know how she looks. That birth announcement was so clever, darling, everyone was so tickled at it, not the least, old Estill.

Even if a P-38 was more a fighter than a bomber, Bischoff flawlessly interpreted my story of the baby shoe and the flying helmet. If a scrap of parachute silk survived, why not a baby shoe? I hoped for that but was content to hold the image of my father attaching my baby shoe to his helmet and flying into the clouds while considering his pending fatherhood. Ernst translated Bischoff's article into English, and it remains easily my favorite. It speaks to the attentive concern of the reporter. My father and his daughter were honored.

In the weeks in Germany, East and West, I gathered new threads into the fabric of my father's story. I knew when I planned this hopeful itinerary that I would want to collect the last missing impressions of my father's life before his fateful flight in April 1945. That included a visit to the American War Cemetery in Margraten, Holland, and a last attempt of three to find the elusive, now demolished, Château le Beauchêne. Enfolded in those plans was my primary agenda, which was to learn the procedure to have a bronze rosette placed next to my father's name on the Tablets of the Missing in the American Cemetery in Margraten. When I noticed the rosettes on my last trip with Hans-Guenther, I wondered what it felt like to know what happened. There is no cachet inherent in living without answers—the rosettes placed beside those names designate a solemn resolution of doubt. I wanted that resolution.

It was a very different visit this time to Margraten. I brought two cream and peach roses with pink petal tips—from my mother and me. I placed them below my father's name on the Tablets of the Missing.

For me, war cemeteries evoke conflicting feelings. It is impossible not to be impressed with their sheer symmetry. The geometric possibilities, to say nothing of the advanced planning, plotting, and planting necessary to achieve this result, are endless and astonishing. The Wall with the names of the unfound is cause for humility in the shadow of their simple inscription:

Lt. Shannon Eugene Estill, Iowa, April 13, 1945

Each inscription is individual but identical. The first time, I made a tracing of my father's name as I've seen people do at the Vietnam wall. I hoped to one day know what happened to him. This time, my father was no longer missing. It was there, in that orderly place—everything aligned and suspended in black marble—that I sensed the sacred passage of time and the accomplishment at Elsnig.

I ventured onto the field of endless crosses to put another bouquet at the site of a friend's uncle. I stopped at the gravesites of the others from my father's squadron and fighter group. Hans-Guenther kindly provided a list of each man from the group and found our way to the crosses. I recognized some of the names from my father's letters. He flew and died with friends.

Amidst my conflicting feelings lay a paradox in that Margraten experience. Though a sense of extreme order and beauty exists in the place—everything is, by design, perfectly symmetrical—I recognized the contradiction. The evidence found in the dirt of the humble Elsnig field belied this sense of perfection and peace. It told the backstory to what I saw at Margraten. Elsnig was the reality, the event, the coming apart of a life with the concurrent ripple across time for all generations who follow. The field in Elsnig held the evidence of catastrophic violence wherein everything was destroyed beyond ordinary recognition—obliterated or reduced to its most common denominator—pieces, rubble, and melt. It was as shocking and horrific as all war deaths.

As I stood entranced by the wavy patterns in the planned order of the Margraten Cemetery, I saw it as a split screen: on one side, the measured order of Margraten's endless crosses; on the other, the shattered reality of each person buried there.

Perhaps because I had just come from the other side of the screen, I felt the injustice of war. Why are we still going to war? Haven't we learned that this is the inevitable outcome? Why is this still acceptable? The names of the people who are buried there, and those who are not, all became as important to me as my father's name listed among them. As if I heard a collective sigh, I told them they were not forgotten. The sad truth is that I never knew that my father's name was even *on* the wall at Margraten. When I found the men of his squadron, they had been sending flowers to Margraten in his name for decades.

FROM CHÂTEAU LE BEAUCHÊNE TO SALT LAKE CITY

From Margraten, we made a trip to Belgium in search of the chateau, the abbey, and the airfield. Château le Beauchêne was just a few kilometers (within walking distance, according to my father) from the village of Falaën. Falaën was the home of Louie's Pub, where my father's squadron (known locally as the "garçons sauvages," or the "wild boys") spent endless hours and Belgian francs. Haircuts were also available.

We arrived in Falaën, and one of two men on the street knew exactly where the chateau was located when it existed. He immediately led us into the woods, telling us that the entry was just beyond the remaining half-gate. The chateau had overlooked a field that has become a 60-year-old forest.

I walked down the road that was certainly the same road my father and his squadron mates walked to Louie's or to the abbey. Certainly, their transport trucks took them to their airfield from that same road. I felt the collision of recognition and familiarity as if my father were walking with me.

The detailed maps with their artful diagrams and descriptions, drawn for me by Jack Zaverl, matched the property where we stood.

Next, we visited Abbaye des Moniales Bénédictines de Maredret, where my father attended Catholic Mass and befriended the resident nuns throughout his stay at the chateau. He wrote often of his visits to the Abbey.

Louie's has been sold to a new owner who may or may not remember the Geyser Gang of the 428th Fighter Squadron. Though the facade of the place has changed, there was a small garage to the right of the entrance that read "Garage Louis" in pale blue letters.

The surprise excursion of the day was at the suggestion of Hans-Guenther, who wanted to show us another special place. We wound our way from the Abbey to Florennes Airfield, known as A78 during WWII. He wanted me to see what remained of the airfield from which my father and his squadron flew their missions. Florennes Air Base (ICAO: EBFS) is a Belgian Air Component military airfield located in Florennes, a municipality of Belgium. It is home to the Second Tactical Wing, operating F-16 Fighting Falcons. It remains a viable air base today, albeit one with deep historical significance.

We managed to gain access onto the base to visit the Spitfire Museum. The display cases surrounding a pristine Spitfire contained photographs and acknowledgment of the presence in the late 1940s of the 474th USAAC Fighter Group. The 474th squadron's Disney-designed insignia were there along with photos of anyone who had contributed to the display. I presented a photo of my father to the museum curator and asked that it be placed in the display as the last man killed from his squadron and a former MIA, now found. They offered to make an entire page about my father in the memory books they keep there. A good day made better by the unexpected.

From there, my next stop was the 17th Reunion of the 474th Fighter Group in Salt Lake City, Utah.

Field Notes, 9/20/2005—*I'm beginning to realize I'm not in Elsnig any more. My laundry has been washed in the machine (rather than nightly by hand; my mother would be proud and astonished at my domestic ability); papers are sorted and filed; my suitcases are back in storage (for a week); I don't awaken at night wondering where the bathroom is in this hotel room; my desk is clear; thank-you notes have been written; Team Estill hats have been distributed; my summer clothes have been swapped for winter in tribute to below 90-degree weather in Arizona; I have made the rounds of my favorite restaurants; I drink iced tea again every day; my dog and cat expect me to feed them now that they remember my true purpose in their lives; and 20 pounds of Haribo Gummi Bears have been divided and distributed (but for the Happy Cherries, which are mine).*

Though I barely had time to contemplate the impact of all I saw, felt, and did in Germany, I had started another kind of excavation: the discovery of feelings and conclusions. It was hard not to get mired in the minutiae of daily living and resort to "thinking about it" without writing about it.

The 474th Fighter Group reunion in Salt Lake City was the perfect venue to tell the story of the Elsnig field—to connect with the people who knew my father then and who were there when he left on his last mission. The relationships I have with my adopted fathers of the 474th are precious and strong. For me, this reunion brought comfort, joy, and that undeniable sense of being loved, validated, and supported. If I ever doubted that this story must be told, I was reminded as I spoke to the group that this story isn't just mine but a part of a collective history and a tribute to everyone who knows the impact of war.

There were a few fewer than 200 of us in attendance. Honorary dad Lloyd Wenzel—our secretary, speaker, and organizer-rainmaker—told us that more than 600 attended the original reunions. When I found them in the very early 1990s, I found 150 of my adopted dads. Time and war have taken their toll on the membership.

This was the first reunion without my most honorary dad, Bill Capron. When I first met Bill, he told me about a baby pool the squadron had started to guess my weight, length, gender, and time and date of birth. Many of the guys remembered the pool and said they never found out who won as my father was killed so shortly after he received the telegram announcing my arrival. He wrote of the infamous baby pool in a letter:

2/13/1945

Hi Sweetie: Just listen to this: We had an impromptu party out here the other nite to welcome a couple of the boys just back from the states. Even I will admit it was pretty drunk out, but everyone had a fine time. During the evening, a couple of the more sober lads dreamed up a scheme to enlarge the bar fund and this is it. A chance to guess the wee Estill's weight at birth (on a scale in 2 ounce graduations from 5#6 oz. to 9#—heaven forbid) can be had for just 25 francs, which is approximately 60 cents. Oh yes, to further increase the element of chance, there will be boy and girl weights. The lucky winner shall be presented with a quart of genuine cognac. WE, of course, get to keep the baby. Soooo my little angel, shoot the exact weight along as soon as possible, huh? The balance of the money we shall use for a baby celebration.

Every man in the 428th is worrying with me about the baby's arrival. I'll wager that ours is the first baby paying for its own celebration. How can that infant be less than a genius with such a financial wizard for a Pop?

I spent the majority of my 10-hour flight home from Germany preparing 42 PowerPoint slides that told "the rest of the story" of my father's last flight. I told them that Tom Wolfe must have been thinking of them when he wrote,

> *The right stuff is not bravery in the simple sense; it is bravery in the most sophisticated sense. Any fool can put his hide on the line and throw his life away in the process. The idea is to be able to put your hide on the line—and then to have the moxie, the reflexes, the talent, the experience, to pull it back at the last yawning moment and then be able to go out again the next day and do it all over again and in its best expression, to be able to do it in some higher cause, in some calling that means something.*

This reunion, like all the others, was sweet and inspiring. Their war stories were poignant, their step a bit slower, but they remembered how it was then and probably how to fly a P-38. Making a presentation to this group was humbling. Despite the presence of the usual Spiegel TV lights and cameras, I was able to give them an overview of our work at Elsnig. I brought a Team Estill flag for them to sign along with labeled P-38 parts for them to touch. As I spoke, I sensed my father's presence there along with his squadron friends who are no longer with us. They were my best audience.

BRINGING LIEUTENANT
ESTILL HOME

The bones of my father were carried by the team who excavated his crash site to the lab at the Joint POW/MIA Command at Hickam Air Force Base in Hawaii. Less than a month after leaving Germany, I was traveling a parallel path from my father's field in Elsnig to welcome him home. In the process and as part of the ritual of repatriation, some of the members of Team Estill and the Spiegel TV film crew would reunite and bear witness to Lt. Estill's return. This repatriation was the first of two ceremonies before he would be buried at Arlington National Cemetery.

Field Notes, 10/11/2005—*How would it be if Mom were still here? She would have lost two husbands, three babies, her parents, her siblings, a daughter, and a granddaughter, but her long-lost husband would be coming home. I'd like to think that she would come with me to Hawaii—we took her there once, and she loved sitting in the sun with her book.*

I've envisioned the scene in Hawaii, I tell her. It will happen on a runway—how appropriate, how circular, how like my father, the pilot. We laugh, but we are sad, and I feel scared. I admit to her that once I've gotten to the part of the story where everything is going my way, falling into place, coming together, I face the emotions that simmer—the unspent ones. It's as if I get emotionally depleted because it takes so long to arrive at that final point, but they are waiting like grief waits with no expiration timestamp.

I have a sense that this event of "repatriation" will be big and powerful and that the imagery will evoke those emotions far more than even the process of digging up the plane and remains. She touches my face: "Honey, it will be okay." Who is the bravest woman on this flight to Hawaii to witness his return?

When my father's plane was shot down by German anti-aircraft fire five months after he arrived in Europe, our family was told that we would never know what happened on that day, much less expect to have him returned to us. And there I was, standing at Hickam Air Force Base, waiting on the runway for my father to be placed reverently on American soil once again.

It was a beautiful Honolulu morning, not yet as humid as it would become, but Hickam is stunning with history and pristine beauty regardless of the weather. I had received the fully escorted tour of JPAC the day before, which included a visit to the famous Central Identification Lab. Among the people I met again who have been essential to the success of my search and recovery efforts was my dear, patient friend and lifeline to JPAC, Johnie Webb. For me, he is to JPAC what Hans-Guenther is to aircraft parts. After being welcomed by him with a big Texas hug, the first thing he told me was that my father's name would soon be added to the Homecoming Commemoration Wall behind us. It was filled with tiny brass nameplates of the 1300 formerly missing that JPAC had identified and returned home. Each tiny plaque represented a life story, and my father's is one of them.

I have always been fascinated by forensics; I suppose that is why I find the study of people so endlessly fascinating. We are not so different in death, I noticed as I observed the bones in the JPAC lab—only more quiet. There is definitely an energy emanating from them in their perfect state of protection behind the glass walls of the identification lab. On that day, about 1,100 active and inactive cases were cataloged and stored there, many of them unsolvable. The table holding the familiar results of our work in the Elsnig field was the second from the front on the far right. The bones and small things we found appeared as a shimmering mirage through the glass. I saw them first in the sifted dirt in Elsnig. I knew them intimately, and I recognized them as my legacy and responsibility. The other tables were heavy with nearly whole skeletons. Bones are the honored guests here, and attention to detail and security for these precious remains is an obvious and serious part of JPAC's work.

The ever-present Spiegel TV crew—Christopher, Theo, and Phillip—had braved a 30-hour nightmare in flying and lost luggage to join me in Hawaii and were already filming and setting up interviews. I tried to string together cohesive answers to Christopher's questions, but the experience of being at JPAC, seeing the famous lab, and being with my father's remains again was overriding any logic or continuity. The team in Elsnig had warned me that this place, representing the reclamation of the indescribable results of death in war, would be humbling. It was that and more.

I've seen many of the world's wonders, but the Central Identification Lab is among the most wonderful. Tender exacting work is done there with highest respect and consideration. Their business is to name the long dead and lost and connect them, as possible, to those who wait. Hope and joy coexist with death and loss. These are the seekers of the messages in the bones and identifiers of the artifacts of a life. Everyone should visit there at least once to consider mortality, if nothing else.

After visiting the lab, I met with historian Chris McDermott, who met us at the field in Germany. In the JPAC archives, he introduced me to his wife, Heather Harris, who is the goddess of all saved things. Heather told me that the archival boxes of files she curated represented each case and asked if I would like to see my father's file.

His now-familiar deceased file was in the beige box identified by his Missing Air Crew Report (MACR). As always, these collections of obscure information tend to include something new, just when I think I've found it all. What was news to me this time was that my father wore a size 10.5 shoe, had his appendix and three wisdom teeth removed, and was 5'11" (though his mother always claimed he was at least six-feet tall). Those things are precious to know, but I also saw the original typed correspondence written by my mother and my grandfather begging the government for information about my father. Each of their letters was attached to the same vague response: "We regret that no further information is available about your husband/son, and if/when we learn something new, you will be informed. No grave/body has been found, and he is considered missing/killed in action." My family couldn't call that reassurance, but it was how they finally accepted their loss. Reluctantly, they closed the door but not their hearts to the possibility that he would be found.

The repatriation ceremony was to begin at 0900 the next morning, Friday, October 21. The Spiegel TV crew drove us to Hickam so they could get a "How are you feeling about today's ceremony?" interview while I was a captive audience. I realized that I was at a loss to name what I was feeling except to offer up the following: happy, sad, proud, delighted, excited, anticipatory, joyous, near tears, in tears, hopeful, and all emotions connected to what some people like to call closure. I called it something else but not closure, because what is ever a closed circle, even in death? Everything is on a continuum. This enabled me to realize that my father's bravery and my love for him brought us all to this place in time. I was grateful to whatever forces made this possible—genetic, angelic, magical, ethereal, or governmental.

We navigated the full parking lot near the runway where the ceremony would happen. Awaiting us in the first parking space, reserved for Dr. Sharon Estill Taylor (daughters have privilege), was a JPAC contingent including Johnie Webb and PR officer Major Nelson-Green. The airfield was crowded with uniformed people, including two veterans groups representing Vietnam and Korea, everyone who works at JPAC who wasn't in the field, and several hundred civilians. I was delighted and surprised to see Rodney Acasio and Shane Bellis, the only two from the Elsnig excavation team who weren't away on the next mission. They had a major part in the reason we were there. They knew it, and so did I. Another gift to me from JPAC.

An enormous C-130 transport plane was parked on the runway. Johnie Webb asked me if I wanted to go aboard to spend a few minutes before the ceremony with my father's transport case that looked like a casket. As we walked up the metal ramp into the open bay, I saw a wash of red, silver, and blue. The red harnesses and seats attached to the walls of the plane exactly matched the stripes on the flags fitted around three silver transport cases holding the remains of the repatriated. The flag-draped transport case that held my father's carefully collected and sifted remains was the middle of three. The other two flags covered the remains of men killed in Vietnam and Laos. My father was no longer alone in a field in Germany but in the company of heroes who followed him. It seemed, at that moment, that we were finally together.

The scene before me offered the impression of colors, stillness, and finality. The Spiegel TV crew remained at the back of the bay as I cautiously approached this long-awaited hard evidence that my mother and my father's family never had.

As I touched the silver box holding my father's remains, I felt only deep sadness at the injustice of his death. All the patriotic logic we had attached to why he died and for what cause momentarily disappeared. Yet, I knew, despite my sadness, that my father's flag-draped presence represented all war losses and that it was what informed my life and shaped my destiny. I was reminded that those of us who experience losing a loved one in war share a fragile bond made of pride and certainty, despite our pain. It's always nice to glimpse your life's purpose.

As we took our places under the VIP canopy for the ceremony, the transport plane was to our left, and on the right, a blue medevac bus waited to take the precious flag-draped boxes back to the lab. JPAC's Commanding General and five other commanding officers marched into the space between, following the uniformed honor guard. We stood at attention three times while my father's military brothers and sisters saluted each flag-draped life as it was carried from plane to bus. My job was to keep breathing and remain present in the moment.

The men who would bear my father's remains entered the open bay for the second time and reappeared carrying the second silver box between them. Though all the flag-draped cases were identical, this one was definitely mine. I stood with my hand on my heart and welcomed my father home.

The last transport case took its place in the bus and the doors were ceremoniously closed. A soldier stood at attention in front of the closed doors and very slowly raised his arm into a perfect salute. A long-awaited moment stopped time. Then I remembered to breathe.

A small cadre of Vietnam vets carried the black silhouette of the MIA/KIA flag flying that day for my father for the last time. He had been found and brought home, and though he will forever be "killed in action," he is no longer left behind.

Photographs of that morning fall short of the sense of honor present in the event. The same reverence and attention to detail is customary with JPAC and has been present in all of my dealings with them. When I met General Flowers (a fellow University of Kansas grad), I said that he could be very proud of the people who are JPAC. His reply was, "I am, and thank you for letting us help you bring your father home."

When we brought JPAC to the crash site a few years ago, I had no illusion that our discovery would supersede any of the other JPAC cases. But what I received as I waited my turn (sometimes not patiently) was copious information, support when I needed it, and the friendship of people who fully understood my mission, because it was their mission too. This ceremony that JPAC gave my father in Hawaii was a dress rehearsal for Arlington in 2006.

I have always been a fortunate girl. The dad who stepped in to raise me used to say that I would fall into shit and come out smelling like a rose. There have been a few times when things weren't always rosy, but this wasn't one of them. I believe that next to the wound is the lesson and opportunity. That's all I did here—look beyond the obvious, disbelieve what I was told to accept as truth, and create the reality in which I would bring my father home.

Field Notes, 10/22/2005—*What remains now? Nothing compares to evidence, forensics, finality, DNA, pieces of a man. Flat facts, but not my father. I am no closer to having him because I have his precious bones. That would have made Nana Lettie sad. No mother should witness that, nor should a daughter, unless it's imperative and important. There's no way to wrap a full man* *around this paltry evidence as to project the image he wore so well for such a short time. They are the stand-ins meant to drive home the final bolt on the locks of the past. They create finality and certainty among speculation and a story. The bones of my father live in my mind's eye now. They are mine; I can hold them if I want—I can string them together like a holy necklace of time and space. I can burn them, scatter them, or keep them under glass, but I know that they belong in home soil, and enough has happened to him without further sullying this lost evidence of his brief life.*

In the bay of the transport plane and not in the field in Germany or ever before, I felt the flag-draped significance of what I had accomplished. I realized that the small bones placed in the special bucket on the German field made real his presence as my phantom father.

The next stop for the repatriated remains was to return them to the Central Identification Laboratory. JPAC forensic scientists, led by Scientific Director Dr. Thomas Holland, would normally begin the final identification process. In this case, the determination had already been made, due to having a matrilineal DNA sample provided by my father's sister. The sample taken from the first bone that appeared in shallow soil at Elsnig in March 2003 was matched with my aunt Margie's DNA sample to determine that we had indeed found Lt. Estill. No amount of blood samples from anyone but a woman from his immediate family could connect the DNA strands so definitively.

Field Notes, 10/22/2005—*What does a writer do when words won't attach themselves to emotions? I have only the constant shuffle of images in my head—images and impressions of a C-31 transport plane carrying three flag-draped transport cases, splendid silver covered in blue and red. Silver like Nana's strong box that kept the letters for me, silver like his P-38 Lightning, silver like the 88 mm anti-aircraft gun that took him away from* *us. The C-31 was built to hold 33 transport cases carrying the broken remains of 33 heroes—heroes despite the nobility of intention or folly of war itself. I climbed up the ramp with my husband and Johnie Webb, both of whom kept me grounded for that last walk to claim my father. Without those two men, then and in the months before, I had a tendency to float above the earth.*

In the hunt for the connection between words and feelings, experiences and images, the connective tissue was awe and sadness, loss and discovery, an accomplishment coupled with exhaustion, pride, and realization that, for all I know, I still don't have him. Yet there he was beneath one of the flags in the belly of that airplane. Here was my father's casket—not the final and official one that would come later as the official burial box, but a representative icon nonetheless. In this form, I felt the certainty of my father's presence and absence all at once. I looked for and found him—I sought his comfort in another silver box.

My life as his daughter has been molded in silver, carved from the earth, and saved in nesting boxes of truth, loss, and revelation. The very smallest one, the one that is the size and shape of a teardrop, holds the key. The key unlocks the silver door impenetrable by human bargaining. It opens only at the request of an honest and weary soul who declares herself ready to walk through it. Until then, it's the only thing stopping me from crossing the bridge or heading in the opposite direction.

Today, in the somber light of the C-31 hold, I touched that door, and I felt the possibility of inward movement. I sensed that within myself a latch had clicked. I was ready and willing to go beyond what I've always known or perceived. It's not scary, and it's not irretrievable or reversible—it's another level of being in the world and accepting the ending of this era called the father-quest. My four children have produced grandchildren who may or may not remember their Nana's mythological quest. I am hopeful there may be one among them who will receive this story and value it for what it is. Meanwhile, I continue to walk the path carrying my father's bright light toward a place where I will make peace with the events of April 13, 1945.

A CEREMONY, ID PACKETS, REVELATIONS, CHOICES, AND WHAT REMAINS

Field Notes, 4/4/2006—*My father comes home to me on Friday. I have no idea what gift my mind will offer my heart on that day. I can only guess it will be profound and that I will feel the impact of his presence and absence in a new way. Another piece of the ongoing saga will manifest. It's strange what is remembered—the awareness of distance and space—what things are behind cupboard doors, on distant shelves, preserved within the scheme of things.*

My father's arrival at my home involved another military ceremony, another step in his daughter's journey. Into this incremental, sentimental story of lifelong patience, I added a new chapter. It was no longer possible to keep it as private grief or to hold it as the heart's history, as it is the true story of a lost and found father. It tells itself as it always has through his letters, which were the breadcrumbs along the path and the validation of what we learned that connected him to the evidence. He has been my collaborator from my first trip with

Hans-Guenther to make this day possible. Thus, it all became real rather than remaining speculation and fantasy. There will never be a way to bring back time and do much but imagine the possible man, but my solace lay in the fact that he was no longer alone in foreign soil. The father I welcomed home was the gift I gave my parents, his family, my family, and myself. It fulfilled the promise I made to my Nana Lettie so she wouldn't cry. While it's true this could have gone undone or without success, the message is that the impossible just takes a little longer.

The military ceremony was a necessary and holy transition. While part of what honors my father, it also illuminated the wonder and mystery that began in 1945. For a brief time, my mother was a hopeful young woman, certain she would live out her life with her young husband and daughter. His final stop would be at Arlington National Cemetery, but this was my chance to have him with me for the first and last time.

To accomplish this, I stood in line with patience, persistence, tireless investigation, suspension of disbelief, and the passage of 60 years plus 358 days to write those words.

I am often asked why I "did that"—I presume "that" means working in the dirt where my father died. The short answer is that I did "that" because it was my legacy and responsibility, and because it wasn't worse than living a life wondering what happened at 1:40 p.m. on Friday, April 13, 1945. I held only the slimmest romantic notion that my father had somehow eluded his certain fate. I'd spent too much time and energy with aircraft recovery experts by that time to believe he had been rescued or now lived in anonymity with soap-opera amnesia somewhere in Tuscany. That was my favorite fantasy but one quickly relinquished after visiting a few unrelated crash sites where it became evident that we were searching for evidence of a catastrophic plane disaster. My father's escape, no matter how I wanted it to be true, was the folly of my romantic wish.

Who can truly blame the daughter of a classic romantic for being romantic?

My mother always told me with absolute conviction that if my father was alive somewhere in the world that he would find a way to come back to us. She even debunked the odd periodic rumor that he had been captured as a spy. Even then, she said, he would have found a way to tell her he was alive. I had no choice but to believe her, thus fueling this passionate mission to find out what actually happened to my father, no matter how grim the details.

In the end, those exact details, enlightening but sobering, were about what we expected in my mother's heartbreaking reality school. What remained of my father was a small collection of bones and objects—modest and somber—a life ended tragically in opposition to the sweet, beautiful, and vibrant way he lived. All of this is now enclosed in a lovely wooden box—an urn, but not in the way I envisioned an urn. This one has a brass plate on the front inscribed with the raised seal of the US Army. The smaller plaque beneath read as follows:

Shannon Eugene Estill
June 26, 1922
April 13, 1945
1st Lieutenant US Army Air Corps*

*Originally, this line said US Army, but I respectfully reminded the US Army that my father flew for the US Army Air Corps, so they sent a replacement posthaste.

For my father's last official homecoming ceremony, I asked JPAC to appoint a member of the German excavation team as the courier for this mission. The first and most insistent person to volunteer was SSG Glenndale Williams, with whom I shared many hours sifting the soil of that Elsnig field and learning to appreciate rap music.

SSG Williams, exactly my father's last age, carried with him, as my father did, the brilliant light of possible heroism, humor, military dignity, and high capability. He was a young man of generous soul and spirit with the bearing of a proud soldier—with a truly incomparable magic smile. Also, he looked gorgeous in his uniform. When you meet for weeks in the dirt of a field in an uncharacteristically hot October in Germany, nobody wears medals or starched shirts. SSG Williams will forever be connected in my mind and memory to this homecoming. My father saluted him on that day, as did legions of fallen soldiers before him.

As luck and fortuitous timing had it, my dear friend Thomas Humphrey was also with me that day. He was on his way to Los Angeles to complete two months of training as a Bikram Yoga instructor. He and I survived graduate school a mere 11 years prior and then together managed an adolescent addiction recovery unit in a Kansas City hospital. I realized recently that Thomas has been with me at every major family event since.

My youngest son, Justin, took time from being an art student at Arizona State University to be with me. It was apparent that he's cut from the same adventurous and creative cloth as his grandfather, and he excels in the son department, as did his grandfather before him.

Those who were with me but unseen were crowded in the entryway watching the transfer of my father's remains. Among them were my mother, of course, smiling and telling me she was proud of me; my father's parents, my Nana and Banka Estill; his grandparents; others who died in all wars before and since who held the same certainty of purpose; and countless others who have missed him dearly for six decades. But, nearest and dearest to me on that day from the ethereal realm was my sister, Chris Waters, who somehow arranged for my father to be returned to me on nearly the exact anniversary of her death one year earlier. Thanks, Chrissy.

Many things occurred to me the morning my father came home. One of them was the awareness gained while working with JPAC in the field and on the army base in Geissen, Germany, that the US military is impressive in many ways, not the least of which in how they memorialize and create ceremony. Where the repatriation in Hawaii was powerful with symbolism and meaning, it was a public occasion. Having my father's remains brought home by a member of the team who helped find him, and having one of my dearest friends and youngest son standing with me, was intimate, bittersweet, and a vision in military excellence.

Earlier that morning, I decided that I would keep the urn on the top shelf of my desk credenza until it was time to deliver it to Arlington National Cemetery. It is the place I keep my father's original art: two of Justin's drawings (one of his pilot grandfather with a little red monkey smoking a cigarette on his shoulder and a pen-and-ink drawing of a P-38 suspended by marionette strings) and a painting of me with my father by artist James B. Hartel. The art of three generations of important artists—my father, my son, and my friend—surrounded my father's memorial box.

Trained well and over time in the ways of Spiegel TV, I hired a film crew to be there, freeing me to simply manage the event from my heart rather than from my head. Cameras were rolling as Major Tony Heigard (a local Army casualty officer) and SSG Williams marched to my front door in flawless military precision with SSG Williams carrying the box, and Major Heigard bearing the folded flag. Such bearing and dignity engenders the grief of the world over time and defines, but doesn't contain, the quiet, insistent power of loss. Nothing manages loss better than, and less than, the passage of time.

SSG Williams presented me with the walnut box, along with a statement of respect and acknowledgment of my father's ultimate sacrifice. As I received the flag from Major Heigard, I handed Justin his grandfather's box of remains so that I could hold the flag and feel the energy that I knew it held along with the price paid for both. Then, we did it all over again for the film crew from every possible angle and nuance of light. It will always be the first, best, and unfilmed take that remains true—receiving the remains of my father that I sought and fought to hold.

My father's uncertain fate was finally known, and the German earth reclaimed what couldn't be salvaged. A part of him, as Dr. Fox said at the last hour of the excavation, will always remain in Germany. What stays constant is the certainty that he deserved to be brought home—if not as the smiling, victorious pilot at the end of the war in 1945, then as the hero he is to me.

That day, I also received the official JPAC Identification packet. It was a comprehensive and fascinating document that determined, in precise detail, my father's identity as the pilot and airplane found in the excavation. It was copious with color photographs, charts, graphs, measurements, descriptions, and baffling DNA analysis but did not include a single photograph of my father in life—a curious oversight.

What we "knew" when we found the crash site years before was based then on hopeful evidence—numbered plane parts, eyewitness accounts of a crash that coincided with what was reported at the time, a growing collection of plane parts, an obvious connection between hope and the coveted facts of discovery. As I listened to the presentation of the conclusions, I marveled at how huge stories and events laden with emotion and drama eventually evolve into flat facts. The ID packet was a stellar example of this evolution. Between two black covers and an ordinary spiral binding was the story I created and lived to tell. Though most of the information was familiar to me, some of it was revelatory. I hadn't realized that we found a piece of his uniform, for instance, and that the maps I watched the anthropologist draw in the field would become stunning computer versions, minus the dirt.

With the ceremony concluded, my thoughts turned to my father's funeral at Arlington National Cemetery. As I soon learned, there were minute details, decisions, and organizational choices to be made. I could have left it all in the capable hands of the Army Casualty Office, but this was difficult to relinquish even into expert hands. However, it was simple compared to what it took to get here. The sound that will be heard at Arlington in October would be that of a circle closing.

I always hoped, and on some level knew, this day of planning would happen. In fact, I counted on it without knowing what would be expected of me or what would be provided. As it turned out, the government provided everything, and my remaining task, on behalf of my father, was to choose dates, guests, and the mode of burial. I had written of my long-standing vision of collecting my father from the field in Germany and bringing him home. When the vision becomes reality, it involves the practicality of caskets and urns—bronze or wood, caisson or hearse. Now or later? It was wartime again, and Arlington was busy.

When I returned from Germany without my father's remains, I wanted him with me, if only briefly, before his final burial in Arlington. Therein lay the symbolic sense of completion and restoration—for him and for me. There's also a proprietary feeling associated with this accomplishment. I am, in essence, claiming my father and assuming my role as his daughter by expressing these wishes and having them granted. I learned that daughters attend to these things when I made similar arrangements in 1991 for my adopted daddy's funeral. I had the same daughterly inclinations and protective feelings. This is what defines my experience of father-loss.

Even as funeral plans were finalized, work continued on the Spiegel TV documentary. The crew who filmed my father's October repatriation ceremony in Hawaii were so moved by the experience that the length of the film was increased and actors were hired for the recreation scenes. We would meet again at Arlington Cemetery in October with the release of the film to the German and US markets scheduled post-funeral and final edits.

In my experience, closure gives way to new, interconnected versions of the same theme. As for this daughter's story, my father's return to me and then to Arlington wrote the final chapter of his life. Nothing could be written without knowing what happened in Germany in 1945. The rest is symbolism and ceremony. My father deserves those things and more, and so do I.

Field Notes, 11/1/2005—*I have all this father stuff tumbling around like words in a dryer. I can see the whirling thoughts, paragraphs, fully formed ideas flying around behind the glass portal in the door, but I have no way to stop the machine and retrieve them. My writing group in Seattle stops the cycle and enables me to sort and arrange my thoughts. Being with this group has unfolded my wings and given me light. Along with all I have accomplished and written on my father's behalf, it makes sense that the first thing I publish is the lead article in* LOST *Magazine, the online offering of editor John Parsley. It is the hologram of my future book. Just a small window of what might be noticed by some fortunate publisher.*

A HERO'S FUNERAL

W hat follows is the story of an event that was never supposed to happen. Considering my geographically divided life and the range of people, surprises, ceremony, and magic I needed to include, whatever is written here will be insignificant compared to what happened.

On Tuesday, October 10, 2006, we celebrated my father's life by honoring him with a full military funeral at Arlington National Cemetery and the Old Post Chapel at Fort Myer, Virginia. When I arrived in Washington before the start of my father's WWII fighter group reunion *and* his funeral, it was amidst driving rain and dark skies.

We headed to Fort Myer and Arlington Cemetery to meet with Leah Rubalcaba from the Fort Myer public relations office. Leah arranged for us to drive the route to my father's gravesite that the funeral procession would take on Tuesday and to visit the actual gravesite. The rain was less persistent, but it had turned colder, and the grass, across which we walked among the endless white markers, was sodden. My father's place there would put him amongst 250,000 brave souls, many of whom died, as he did, in battle while defending our freedom. I didn't like the muddy track of road that ran along the end of that row, but Leah assured me (as she would about a million other things) that it provided only temporary access to new gravesites, and it would eventually be seamlessly connected to the surrounding landscape. This graves section was, in fact, becoming an historic site where a WWI soldier had only recently been buried.

After a final logistical planning session for Tuesday's funeral in the Fort Myer public relations office with the Spiegel TV crew and a visit to the Old Post Chapel where we would have the funeral, Leah drove us back to the hotel.

In the days before the funeral, more and more relatives, friends, and adopted pilot dads arrived. Among them were my former student, teaching and research assistant, and incomparable friend, Jonathan Mackey; my college friend (circa 1964 and beyond) Moreen Rogan McGurk, from Manhattan; my other dear pal (circa 1970) Denise Gibb Schlax, from Chicago; Dr. Deborah Stokes from DC; and my mermaid sistah, Dr. Pat Weyer, from Seattle, along with her mother, Patricia Leigh, from Connecticut. I am blessed with enviable girlfriendships.

By Monday night, my oldest daughter, Andrea Philippart, was there along with oldest son Raymond Bates, daughter-in-law Evelyn, and their kids, Delaney, Alexis, and Noah, from Kansas City. Laura Malinasky brought her son Nick and daughter Emma. Having all my kids in one place is my favorite thing in the world.

We attended the official 474th Fighter Group reunion banquet that night, where Congressman Ike Skelton spoke about the bravery and patriotism of the squadron members present in and absent from that room. We lost many of them that year, including Bill Capron in January and Jack "Radar" Zaverl on my birthday in March. Incomparable men, incredible friends, and brave pilots to the end. I have been blessed with precious and extraordinary friends among my adopted dads of the 474th Fighter Group.

That day, my father's squadron friend Paul Meier told a story I'd never heard about my father. Apparently, seven pilots, including my father, arrived in Paris to await their squadron assignments. They learned they had been assigned to the 474th Fighter Group and the 428th Fighter Squadron in Belgium but that they had been reassigned as ferry pilots. Determined to fly the P-38s they loved, they decided to show up at their squadron with their original orders.

Paul Meier said none of them wanted to be ferry pilots, but he sadly speculated that if my father had taken the ferrying job, he might be alive. In the end, nothing could stand between these pilots and their airplanes—even orders to the contrary. Paul said they figured that good ferry pilots were easier to find than great P-38 pilots.

Parting Words

The day of my father's funeral was sunny from the start. I didn't sleep much that night, so I watched the sunrise over the city and the new Air Force Memorial visible just outside my hotel window. I knew it was a magical day and that whatever happened would be exactly right.

Friend and glass artist Dr. Pat Weyer designed and created a 22-pound glass tribute bowl for the occasion that is hand-etched with my father's wings and a tiny P-38 chasing clouds. On the larger section below is an engraved excerpt from one of my favorite letters, written by my father just days before he died:

Dearest Angels: How I should love to be with you two now.

Must fly again, so good night, and sweet dreams. Gener

The tribute bowl was displayed at the reception at the Fort Myer Officers' Club. Inside the bowl were a dozen smooth, green river rocks engraved with the names of the people in my father's family—his parents, his brother and sister, my family, and, of course, Dr. Pat Weyer. Everyone who attended the funeral had a chance to sign a card with their name if they wished to have a stone placed in the tribute bowl. Everyone did. For me, the day was made more meaningful because of Pat. I am so proud to be her friend and to benefit from not only her artistic offerings but from her wisdom.

Since my father's remains lived with me for six months prior to his burial in Arlington, I was able to open the walnut box provided by the US Army and include a symbolic token with his bones. No photos, business cards, medals, buttons, or other earthly items would carry him into his next life. He knew about all the milestones in my life.

Pat, with whom I transited the murky vortex of our doctoral program, gave me a small, green disk with a stylized white dolphin enameled on one side. She explained it was a psychopomp. The role of a psychopomp is to escort deceased souls into the afterlife, to provide them safe passage. Considering my father's violent death and how long he remained with his plane in Germany, I thought including this token made sense, practically and spiritually. My friendship with Pat is a treasure in my life. From the first time she heard me speak of my father, she completely understood why I needed to find him. We relate as our fathers' daughters and women who have survived great father-loss.

Despite all my worrying in advance, everyone found their way to the Old Post Chapel at Fort Myer, just outside one of the Arlington National Cemetery gates. At the foot of the chapel altar was a small table, upon which my cousin Shannon Estill had placed the portrait of my father that always hung in our grandparents' home. As a little girl, a teenager, and later an adult and mother, I would stand in front of that photo and feel my father's presence. It was my grandmother's favorite, and she never passed it without running her fingers over the glass in a gesture of deep love and inconsolable grief. Now that same portrait hangs in cousin Shannon and his wife Kathi's home. Their daughter, Shayne, has been raised, as I was, under the watchful eyes of my father.

As I looked at that familiar picture of my father, I wondered if I would have the courage to stand up before this gathering crowd to tell them how much I loved this smiling, handsome, young pilot who was my father, my mother's only true love, and the lost crown prince of my grandparent's family.

The weekend rain was replaced by a day resplendent and representative of my father's brief, shining life. My immediate family gathered in the waiting room adjacent to the altar. Those who were there to remember my father were seated in the chapel—his squadron mates, their family and friends, my oldest and dearest friends from around the country, and the nearly dozen Estills, including my father's brother, Wes.

Those who made this funeral possible were Leah Rubalcaba (I swear the woman has wings), who saved me from certain meltdown many times in this process; Paul Bethke, the former boss of JPAC and now the Army Casualty Office's gain; musicians Jerry and Dan, who played music from the 1940s at the reception and don't normally attend the funerals they perform for, though they made an exception in this case; and Alan and Gloria Layne, the former AWON president and my ally in the war against unfounded beliefs and illogical rumors, who also lost her father in WWII.

Also present and very busy was the Spiegel TV crew, performing their intricate dance of camera work and timing while being in at least six places at once. They were, as always, the picture of German efficiency and elegance.

Dennis Kan, the artist who photographed every second of the funeral, provided incomparable photographs that captured each moment of the pageantry and precision of the day. Dennis's generosity was one of the sweetest moments of my life. In all, he gave me nearly 300 photos, refusing to take payment.

At precisely 11:00 a.m., the same soldier who would later carry my father's urn into the chapel escorted me to my seat. (Four-going-on-24 granddaughter Emma asked who was getting married.) It was while walking with the soldier that surrealism intersected with joy and sorrow. I realized the enormity of what had been accomplished with the support of the mortal and ethereal and how this day, in reality, far exceeded my vision of it. I knew, beyond a doubt, that my father was truly present.

Everyone stood as the box holding my father's remains was brought to the front of the chapel. Though I'd spent countless hours in the presence of that lovely wooden box, it had taken on a new energy in the hands of the soldier who held it. He placed it on the little table next to the portrait of my smiling father, and ANC Chaplain Creamer took his place at the podium. The funeral, long awaited and planned, had begun. He welcomed everyone and then introduced Reverend Brad Collins, the chaplain of the 474th Fighter Group and one of my father's squadron mates in Belgium and Germany.

Reverend Brad was the spiritual inspiration for the dwindling troops of the 474th and attended every reunion I attended and more before that. He always inspired me with his carefully chosen words of inspiration at our banquets and ceremonies. His presence exemplified the phrase "man of God." When asked to officiate at my father's funeral, he agreed without hesitation. Everyone present that day and in his worship community in California knows he was a treasure. He spoke lovingly of Lt. Shannon Estill and of his place in the squadron and how the loss of one of them was the irreparable loss of family.

Since it fell to me to give my father's eulogy, I considered my parents' correspondence that illuminates their life together. In that spirit, I wrote my father a letter that I would l read. It wasn't the first, nor will it be the last letter I write to him, but it was the first public reading. I've found comfort and answers to hard questions in this letter-writing practice, and I wanted to tell him a few things on this day.

At first it was difficult to read the names of those who are already with him—his parents and grandparents; my mother; my sister, Chris Waters; and our son-in-law, Brian Olson; among others. The next names I read were of those to whom I owed the success and realization of the day. Thereafter, I entered a zone of certainty that what I'd written was incidental to what I felt. I hoped my feelings would carry me through to reading the Thomas Lynch poem "Kisses" at the end. In a few lovely lines, the poem captures the essence of what I feel about my parents. It's as if the poet wrote it with them in mind, though he later told me he wrote it for his parents.

Kisses

My father turns up in a dream

Sometimes on roller skates,
Sometimes in wing-tipped shoes

He's smiling
Impeccably dressed

Himself again

I am delighted to see him

Maybe I was only dreaming is what I tell myself inside the dream.

No, he assures me wordlessly
The facts are still the facts

He's dead.

He and my mother have been to the movies

She's gone on ahead of him to make the coffee

He lets me hold him
hug him,
Weep some
Awake repaired again

He says he'll take my kisses home to her.

I returned to my seat after reading my letter, feeling proud and relieved. My husband, Paul, sang "Let There Be Peace on Earth," a song we chose for our wedding in 1973. As I heard it again, I had renewed admiration for and awareness of Paul's musical gifts as he makes it sound effortless and elegant, the way people with innate gifts often do.

Our son, Justin, followed his father to the altar to read Gillespie Magee's poem "High Flight." My grandmother read it to me as a child, and I was later given a framed copy by Jack Zaverl. To hear it read by my son at the funeral of his grandfather gave it even deeper meaning. I will always associate "touching the face of God" with my father and the pilots before and since who have "slipped the surly bonds of earth."

A Long, Meaningful Walk

At exactly 11:30 a.m., my father was taken from the chapel and into the brilliant day. A flag-draped casket on a caisson with six black horses, one without a rider, waited for him. His box was placed in a casket, and the final walk to the gravesite began. It was the last full mile of this long and loving journey for me, and the last moments my father would spend suspended in time and place. I was, finally and proudly, walking him home.

I knew then, as I know now, that my father's spirit may always be divided between the field in Germany and Arlington

Cemetery. That last walk behind his casket represented the integration of those two realities. It would never have been enough to leave him in Germany, even though the people of that sweet village now know the name of the American pilot who rested in their field for nearly 62 years. In the end, I knew that my father should be among his courageous comrades here at home, where his family could always find him.

My grandchildren walked with me in the funeral procession, as did my kids, my husband, my friends from near and far, all my Estill cousins, and everyone else who was able and knew, as I did, that we walked with purpose and in honor of my father. In reflecting upon the scene, preserved so perfectly in Dennis Ken's photographs, I see my cousin Wes carrying the framed photograph of my father. It reminded me of the families of the disappeared walking to protest the unknown fate of their loved ones. I thought of how long my father was among the disappeared and how far this day went toward making him visible to us!

As we arrived at the gravesite, flying above us, in perfect tribute to my father, were two magnificent A10 Thunderbolt Warthogs, among our country's finest and fastest warplanes. I wondered who the pilots were and if they knew how much it meant to us to see them in heir splendid formation. I wrote them a letter of deep gratitude when I returned home, telling them that my father could never have envisioned such glorious evolution in flight.

We gathered where my father's box was placed on a small, draped table. Behind the table were white crosses far into the distance. All that remained was to watch the precise ritual of folding and presenting the flag.

My Uncle Wes sat next to me holding my father's photograph and my hand. Occasionally, he leaned over and whispered that he loved me. I told him that I loved him too and that my father was finally home. He and my Aunt Margie knew my father in a way I never could, and they were where his spirit resides for me in real time. To have my Uncle Wes next to me at that moment was the representation of everything I love about my family of birth. Many people expended tremendous effort to bring my uncle to be with us at Arlington that day, and they did it with the certainty that his presence would add immeasurably to our sense of family. He was our patriarch. His presence was the expression of love by his seven children who, in the time-honored Estill tradition, take care of each other forever.

Reverend Brad read his final blessing, which far exceeded my expectations. In fact, the entire day was more than everything I imagined, and from a far higher order of existence. The flag that had been on top of the casket was folded by two lines of decorated soldiers and presented to me by Chaplain Creamer. It was preserved in the flag case I received from Lt. Col. Roxanne Austin, the DC casualty assistance officer. It reminds me of my father's memorial box—smooth, polished wood with the US Army seal on the outside above a plaque with my father's name. His medals and a replica of his silver wings are affixed to the inside lid.

I stayed at the gravesite until my father's remains were in the ground. I was privileged to participate in taking him out of the ground in Germany, and I intended to witness his long-awaited transition into American soil. I took a single rose from the massive bouquet at the gravesite and placed it in the grave. I sent him my love and my wish that he be with my mother and that he find spiritual peace in this sacred place. Only then could I leave him.

History Corrected

By the time I arrived at the luncheon reception at Fort Myer Officers' Club, everyone was enjoying lunch, great music, and the bittersweet euphoria we all relish at the culmination of historical events.

At the reception, I showed a memorial video I created in 1990 as a vision for the future and a reflection on the past. As always, it moved people to tears but no more than me as my Uncle Wes, who remembered little in present time, identified each person in the old family photographs in the film. He saw his parents, his little sister, himself as a young boy, careening wildly around a corner on one tricycle with his older brother. He said my father was married to a "very sweet girl, and we love her." I didn't watch the video as much as I watched my Uncle Wes travel through time. For some persons with dementia, they have recall of the past but not the present. My uncle was happily living in the 1920s, '30s, and '40s that afternoon.

My work as a Spiegel TV diva wasn't finished. When everyone left Fort Myer, Kay, Theo, and Bastian took me back to my father's gravesite. This would be the last of more than 60 hours filmed over more than three years. I stood at my father's grave alone. By putting the camera on a massive crane brought from Germany and constructed on-site, balanced by cases of water, the film crew could pan over the cemetery in a final sweeping scene.

Then, as though awakening from a complex but lovely dream, it was over. After a final photo with the Spiegel TV team, we were off to visit my father's cenotaph/memorial headstone one last time. It had been placed in the section reserved for the missing in action—two rows up from the memorial marker of my parents' favorite 1940s bandleader Glen Miller. Arlington destroys these markers after burial because those they represent are no longer missing. Arlington Cemetery always needs room for more who have not yet been, or never will be, found.

Time was scarce to talk long enough or in any depth with the people who were there for my father. My dear pal Paul Hissey reminded me to "throttle back," as all good pilots know. It wasn't until I stepped, once again, on the deck of my Pacific Northwest houseboat a week later that I fully understood the meaning of family. I also regretted that I worried at all that this wouldn't be as magnificent a celebration as it was. I should have known by then.

As for my mother, I would like to believe that I had helped to restore and heal her wherever she was with my father. They are together, as they vowed in 1943, for all time.

When I was handed the folded flag from her husband's casket, I would have willingly granted her the privilege of accepting it. After all, I did this because she could not. She died not knowing she had been tricked by society and the cultural dictates of the post-war 1950s into believing that she would never have the answers she needed to live a life of resolution.

By finding my father and bringing him home, I stepped onto the star that was my birthright as a seeker of archetypal truth. In the eternal stillness at Arlington National Cemetery, I was able to correct history and memorialize that truth, not just for me but for my mother.

The relief of completion was sweet. I continue to be blessed by the company of my family, good friends, and the bright possibility of each new day. I don't doubt divine inspiration and the protection of my personal army of angels. Above all, I am grateful to the architects of my journey—my mother and fathers—who gave me wings and taught me how to fly.

THE QUEST CONTINUES

I s this the end of the story? Probably not. Maybe never.
As long as someone wants to hear it, read it, or paint it,
it remains viable and part of me. I am continually asked if
I have "closure," as it is assumed I must or will soon have it.
Usually I am polite and agree that closure is imminent. The
truth is, my educated and instinctive guess is that closure is
elusive and probably nonexistent. New stories, like connected
memories, are already appearing.

On May 25, 2007, I stood in the American Cemetery in
Margraten, Holland. It was an overcast, rainy day with dim
skies that were the antithesis of the brilliant, austere, clear day
in Arlington seven months earlier. Still, I had made a promise
in 2001: to return and place a rosette by my father's name to
mark that he was found and no longer missing. The occasion
was auspicious and solemn in that ceremonious way I have
learned to expect; the cemetery in full bloom even in the drizzle
was energized in anticipation of Memorial Day.

Our smaller but no less significant ceremony had become a press event, and I was scheduled to speak to the media—television, newspaper, and radio—about my father. I agreed in advance that the press and any members of the public visiting the cemetery would be welcome to witness the ceremony. Also in attendance were the mayor of Margraten, the US ambassador to Holland, our Spiegel TV crew, several of my fellow war-orphan siblings, and of course, a few special members of Team Estill Germany, including Hans-Guenther. At my request, he came from the crowd to stand with me as the long-awaited and envisioned rosette was tapped into the wall next to my father's name. We knew how far we'd traveled.

But still, our travels were not complete.

There was, after all, a movie to be seen on local German television.

The film was, in a word, surreal, and also in German. I was privileged to meet Hauke Ketelsen, editor of our film, finally titled *A Love in Time of War: The Last Flight of Lt. Estill*. Throughout the film, excerpts from my father's letters are read, along with reenactments of scenes pertinent to his life and death. Spiegel TV generously translated the film into English for a US audience and for me. They even hired English-speaking actors, so the US version doesn't have subtitles.

Watching the film at Spiegel TV minus the German narration and dialogue and with Kay Siering telling me the story in English gave me a good idea of its impact. It goes far beyond what I could have imagined and is a visible link to my father unlike any other. Since it has been shown worldwide, I receive letters via my website about the film's impact.

The project led to speaking opportunities. In November of 2008, I was invited to speak at the American WWII Orphans Network Conference in Tucson, Arizona. I was thrilled and surprised to be included at this level of importance and to receive a commemorative and appreciative plaque. It was at this conference I fortuitously met Stephen Watson, then-executive vice president and chief operating officer of the National WWII Museum in New Orleans. Stephen suggested that our Spiegel TV film about my father's last flight should be shown at the museum. I told him I loved the idea, but it wasn't up to me—the film belongs to Spiegel TV. I predicted that this could take time.

A decade after film producer Kay Siering called from Germany to ask if I was interested in having a documentary film made about the search for and recovery of my father, we watched its US premiere together. The setting was the National WWII Museum's glorious Solomon Victory Theatre with an overflowing audience. The film was a hope and a wish fulfilled since neither Kay nor I knew how the story would unfold or even if the search would yield anything of interest.

Following the film, we talked with the audience for 45 minutes. This was a discerning group whose questions were astute, considered, and thoughtful. People asked me if I had written the book yet. One question I remember well was whether I was finished with this father-quest. I tried to say yes, but the truth is that there always seems to be one next thing that draws me back.

Just a year later—six years after the excavation in Elsnig—Bob Alvis, president of the P-38 National Association, created a museum case in my father's honor at the Planes of Fame Air Museum in Valle, Arizona, at the south entrance to the Grand Canyon. I donated one of my father's two dress uniform jackets and some of the excavated pieces of his plane. Dayle DeBry, director of air shows, had dog tags made much like the ones my father wore but which were never found at the excavation site. From those few things, they created an incredible museum case that honors my father in the section dedicated to pilots from the 474th. Among those in attendance was 1st Lt. Paul Meier, whose plane my father was flying on April 13, 1945.

That same year, I sponsored an encore performance of Welsh composer Karl Jenkins's composition *The Armed Man: A Mass for Peace*. Commissioned by the Royal Armouries Museum for the Millennium celebrations, Jenkins dedicated the composition to the victims of the Kosovo crisis. The compelling message of war and peace spoke to the purpose of my father's sacrifice. After hearing *The Armed Man*, I knew it told the story of all who have died for peace. On September 27, 2012, *The Armed Man* was performed in honor of my father by InConcert Sierra, in Grass Valley, California, with Ken Hardin directing 66 choristers. Each clipped a photo of my smiling father to their music as they sang for him.

And still, the work is not done. As always, and what has served me well, is to remain active in the creation of my own present and future. To continue in the belief that my father's sweet memory should be honored, along with the memories of all those who died, as he did, in service to our country. I never forget that this story can be told only after paying the highest possible price for the rights to do so.

I still don't believe in "closure" in any traditional sense.

AFTERWORD

Why did I do this? What does this provide besides the thrill of discovery? It's certainly not always appearing on the same stage with sorrow, joy, and the revelation that "my daddy died in the war." My reason is far simpler in its complexity. The truth is that I did it as the curator of my father's legacy. I did it because my mother never could. I did it to honor the fighter pilots who witnessed my father's life and death and never forgot. But above all, I did it so I can be my father's daughter.

I never felt my father's mortal arms around me, saw my parents together, had a sibling with whom I would share them, or heard my father's voice. Instead, I have created resurrection from the wreckage the war made of those things.

I've always believed that the twin losses of my father to war and my first child to adoption are intertwined. While there is never a way to retrieve my father in an earthly sense, that is exactly what I did when I searched for and found my son.

Both were lost to me forever, according to what was accepted custom. I had no reason to expect either would be mine to love or to claim. One to oblivion, the other to a different life. I felt the grief of my father's death on an 18-year delay when I saw my son for the first time. I can only imagine, but never know, what the loss of her first grandchild must have added to my mother's accumulated grief. If I link the two events, the surrender seems identical in its irretrievable nature. The casualty and the loss are the same, and repressed sadness flow beneath both into an ocean of immeasurable distance.

When I left home to find my lost son, it was a similar trip in deliberation and purpose. While it was a pallet of a far different hue, it included exactly the same secret hopes: to find what was lost and bring it home. My father can never stand before me or tell me he loves me. I can do all of that for my once lost and now found son. The war took my father from me; but I found him too. The common thread is my determination and belief that I deserved to know the end of those stories, and my son and my father could not stay out there in the distance without being brought back to where they belong and are most deeply loved.

The letter below was included in the letters saved by my father's mother. It is an undiscovered love letter to me that is part of the unending journey that is my father-quest.

Dearest Daughter,

I write to you from where my squadron is awaiting the new dawn. I should be sleeping, as I have an early flight, but sleep eluded me because I was thinking of you. The announcement of your birth arrived this morning, and I have thought of nothing else since. What must it be like to be a father? Is this it? Should I do something differently now? Get up on the other side of my cot? Whistle when I walk? Pray a little harder for this war to be over? All of the above, I suppose. Meanwhile, I am so proud to know you are in this world, even though I wish it were a safer place to live right now. *That is why I am away from you, my sweet girl, because I have a job to do that will keep you safe in your mother's arms.*

I want this to be the only war of your lifetime. If you'd waited a couple of months to be born, I think you may have missed it altogether. As is, I will have to finish my job over here and then come home and stay forever. I have lots of plans for us that include traveling in our own airplane (I've had a lot of airplane flying practice lately) and maybe starting an airline with Uncle Clark so we can fly people all over the country to visit the people they love. Also, I just want to spend some time looking at you and at your mother. Looking and hugging and telling you both how much I love you.

Well, your Pop will have a new mission today, besides the one the Army Air Corps has in mind. That is, to come home very soon; and when I do, I will be the guy in the uniform running down the street. I'll be saying, "Where's my beautiful daughter? Tell her Daddy's home!" Until then, my lovely girl, I am your devoted POP.

GALLERY 4
BRINGING HIM HOME

Paul Hissey

Howard Darnell

Marilyn Hickock

Raynor Roberts

Lloyd Wenzel

Flag-draped cases in the bay of a C-130 transport plane

1st Lt. Estill's Repatriation

Team Estill reunion in Hawaii with Rodney Acacio and Shawn Bellis

Johnie Webb, Sharon, and Paul Rocca

Dr. Taylor and Dr. Holland at JPAC lab

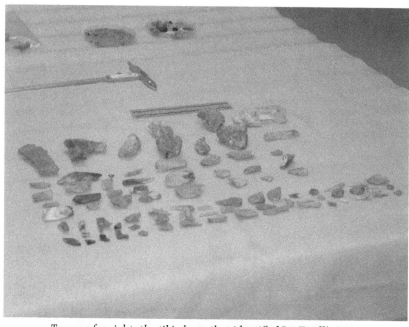

Top row far right, the tibia bone that identified Lt. Estill's DNA

Major Tony Heigard, Justin Rocca, SSG Glenndale Williams

Psychopomp

Tribute Bowl created by Dr. Pat Weyer

Old Post Chapel, Ft. Meyer

The riderless horse

1Lt Shannon Eugene Estill
June 26, 1922 – April 13, 1945

High Flight

Oh! I have slipped the surly bonds of earth
And danced the skies on laughter-silvered wings;
Sunward I've climbed, and joined the tumbling mirth
Of sun-split clouds — and done a hundred things
You have not dreamed of — wheeled and soared and swung
High in the sunlit silence. Hov'ring there
I've chased the shouting wind along, and flung
My eager craft through footless halls of air.
Up, up the long delirious, burning blue,
I've topped the windswept heights with easy grace
Where never lark, or even eagle flew —
And, while with silent lifting mind I've trod
The high untresspassed sanctity of space,
Put out my hand and touched the face of God.

— Pilot Officer Gillespie Magee

Funeral Service and Tribute

BLESSING
Rev. Brad Collins
(428th Squadron)
Chaplain Elect 474th Fighter Group Association

TRIBUTE AND REFLECTIONS
Paul Meier
(428th Squadron)

Sharon Estill Rocca Taylor
Daughter of 1Lt Shannon E. and Mary T. Estill

SONG
Let There be Peace on Earth
Paul G. Rocca
Son-in-law of 1LT Shannon E. and Mary T. Estill

POEM
High Flight
Justin T. Rocca
Grandson of 1Lt. Shannon E. Estill
and Mary T. Estill

PROCESSIONAL TO GRAVESITE

GRAVESIDE BLESSING
Rev. Brad Collins

Reverend Brad Collins leading 1st Lt. Estill into the chapel

Following the caisson between Old Post Chapel and my father's gravesite

Uncle Wes Estill holding his brother's photo

Mission accomplished

From left: Justin Rocca, Raymond and Ev Bates, Nick Malinasky, Andrea Philippart, Laura Mallinasky, Paul Rocca, Alexis Bates, Sharon with grandchildren, Emma Malinasky, Noah, and Delaney Bates

December 2019 Board of Trustees group, Higgins Hotel opening

Mike Ysenchak, Sharon, Hans-Guenther at rosette ceremony

The Rosette for 1st Lt. Estill

With Kay Siering at Spiegel TV headquarters, Hamburg

Sharon and Kay Siering with film posters in English and German

Sharon and Paul Rocca with Spiegel TV crew: Theo Bernd, Kay Siering,
Christopher Gerisch in Hamburg

1st Lt. Estill's memorial brick on walk outside WWII Museum

InConcert Sierra's Master Chorale with conductor Ken Hardin

Planes of Fame Air Museum, Valle, Arizona

Justin Rocca at his grandfather's museum case

Paul Meier and Sharon with the closed case

ACKNOWLEDGMENTS

These were the granters of my wishes who saw value in finding a lost fighter pilot and reuniting him with his daughter. They brought willingness, rare relationships, and course correction. Without them, this book would be a work of fantasy and fiction. As the puzzle deciphering my father's disappearance was assembled, they added the pieces, no matter how obscure, creating a masterpiece. I have gratitude without boundaries for them and for those who watched from a distance. Most are mentioned in the book—all are the heart of this project. This story isn't only mine but part of a collective history and a tribute to everyone who knows the impact of war.

Team Estill Germany
- Hans-Guenther Ploes, Ernst Eberle, and my German sistahs Wally Busch and Traudl Thiel
- JPAC Team Estill in my father's field
- Spiegel TV

- The village of Elsnig, the town of Torgau, and the Torgauer newspaper
- Giessen US Army Base, Giessen, Germany

Team Estill US

- Paul Rocca
- My homefront families: Philippart, Rocca, Malinasky, and Bates
- Jonathan Mackey, LMSW
- 474th Fighter Group; the 428th, 429th, and 430th Squadrons; and all my adopted dads
- Joint POW/MIA Command, Honolulu, HI (DPAA: Defense POW/MIA Accounting Agency)
- P-38 National Association
- American WWII Orphans Network
- Arlington National Cemetery and Leah Rubalcaba
- Stephen Watson, CEO of the National WWII Museum, New Orleans, Los Angeles, and Gordon "Nick" Mueller, CEO emeritus and founder
- InConcert Sierra, Grass Valley, CA
- Planes of Fame Museum, Chino, California, and Valle, Arizona
- Doreen McDonald, whip-smart discerning reader and teaching assistant
- Most glorious Gerda Weissmann Klein who insisted this book be written
- Julian Medina, IT genius
- Holly Peppe, who turned on the second edition light

JPAC Team Estill

- Team Leader: CPT David Emmons
- Team Sergeant: SFC Craig Daniels
- Recovery NCO: SSG Glenndale Williams
- Recovery NCO: SSG Shane Bellis

- Anthropologist: Dr. Greg Fox
- Life Support Analyst: MSG Rodney Acasio
- Linguist: SSG Richard Thomas
- EOD: Marine SSG Jeff Streeter
- Photographer: TSGT Linda Miller

Team Estill Holland

- Margraten American Cemetery and the adopters of the American graves

And, my deepest gratitude for your appreciation of my story and your skill with words and feelings: Jennifer Durrant, Sam Wright and Amy Osmond Cook at Sourced Media Books, LLC, and Osmond Marketing.

ABOUT THE AUTHOR

Sharon Estill Taylor, MSW, PhD, is an educator, speaker, former professor of psychology, social work, and women's studies, and author of two books. Dr. Taylor is a member of the National WWII Museum's Board of Trustees and a frequently invited presenter at conferences, where she speaks about issues of grief, loss, unimaginable wonder, and reinvention.

Her first book, a memoir, *Phantom Son: A Mother's Story of Surrender*, was published in 2015. A Spiegel TV documentary film, *A Love in the Time of War: The Last Flight of Lt. Estill*, chronicles the search for and recovery of her father's WWII crash site in Germany.

She lives in the civilized Sonoran Desert of Arizona near her four children, most of her 10 grandchildren, and in harmony with Dharma, her faithful feline companion.

To learn more about Dr. Taylor and her work, visit her website: myphantomfather.com or sharonestilltaylor.com.

CPSIA information can be obtained
at www.ICGtesting.com
Printed in the USA
LVHW081704070322
712830LV00029B/667/J